SPANISH THEATRE 1920–1995

STRATEGIES IN PROTEST AND IMAGINATION (2)

Contemporary Theatre Review
1998, Vol. 7, Part 3, p. iii
Reprints available directly from the publisher
Photocopying permitted by license only

Contents

Contemporary Theatre Review
1998, Vol. 7, Part 3, pp. 1–23
Reprints available directly from the publisher
Photocopying permitted by license only

Directors of the Twentieth Century Spanish Stage

María Francisca Vilches de Frutos

This article examines the role of the director in the modern Spanish theatre. Beginning with the influence of foreign practitioners on the earliest generation of directors (Valle-Inclán, Adrià Gual, and Rivas Cherif), it moves on to look at the establishment of a National Theatre in the aftermath of the Civil War and the independent groups which sprung up across the country during the latter years of the Franco dictatorship. The final section discusses the directors who emerged from the independent theatre movement to become managers/artistic directors of the public theatres developed after the Socialist Party's arrival to power.

KEY WORDS: Directors, Mise-en-scène, National Theatre, Theatre practice, Plastic arts.

The Beginning: 1898–1939*

There is a widely held view in contemporary historiography that the concept and function of 'metteur en scène' were not considered important in Spanish theatre until recent times.[1] However, any analysis which covers the beginning of the twentieth century indicates precisely the opposite. Works by André Antoine, Adolphe Appia, Stanislavsky, Filippo Marinetti, Romain Rolland, Gordon Craig, Max Reinhardt and Luigi Pirandello were well-known in the 1920s and 1930s. Pirandello,

*My sincere thanks to Mr. José Ibáñez Haro, my research assistant.

[1] César Oliva, '1898–1936: Ocaso de un siglo y amanecer de las vanguardias', in *Escenarios de dos mundos*, II (Madrid: Centro de Documentación Teatral, 1988) and Guillermo Heras Toledo, 'Ausencias y carencias en el discurso de la puesta en escena española de los años 20 y 30', in *El teatro en España entre la tradición y la vanguardia (1918–1939)*, eds. Dru Dougherty and María Francisca Vilches de Frutos (Madrid: Consejo Superior de Investigaciones Científicas, Fundación Federico García Lorca, Tabacalera, S.A., 1992) pp. 139–146. On the contrary see Felipe Higuera, 'La dirección de escena en Madrid (1990–1975)', in *Cuatro siglos de teatro en Madrid*, ed. Andrés Peláez (Madrid: APSEL, 1992), pp. 117–143.

Aurélien Lugné-Poe and George Pitoëff visited Spain during these years with their own companies.[2] The Third Congress of the Universal Theatre Society in Barcelona (20–26 June, 1929)[3] brought together such important directors as Firmin Gémier, Gaston Baty, Paul Blanchard, Leopold Sachse (National Theatre, Hamburg), René Reding (National Theatre, Belgium), and Marinetti. Anton Giulio Bragaglia came to the Students Residence in Madrid, where Federico García Lorca lived and studied, to explain his scenographic concepts. Jacques Copeau also performed Plautus's *Menaechmi* there. Erwin Piscator visited Barcelona in 1936, invited by the Generalitat Government.

Many articles in books and periodicals may be found which criticize the director's role in the staging of a piece in order to confirm his importance in the general theatrical process. In newspapers, famous critics such as Luis Araquistáin, Enrique Díez-Canedo, Manuel Fernández Almagro, Manuel Machado, Rafael Marquina, Enrique de Mesa, Arturo Mori, Manuel Pedroso, Cipriano de Rivas Cherif and Ramón J. Sender developed an extended idea of interdisciplinary theatre as an integration of different art forms. Discussing Antoine's theory they illustrated the difference between theatre as a literary form and theatre as a show. They enhanced the idea of creating the role of 'metteur' and insisted on separating the principal actor's role from the stage director's antithesis of nineteenth century theories. As with Stanislavsky and Craig, they expounded a new method for the performer's role: upholding the modern theories of the 'metteur' and discussing the critical stance of Vsevolod E. Meyerhold, Leopold Jessner, Nikolai N. Evreinov, Jacques Copeau, Aleksandr Y. Tairov, Charles Dullin, Louis Jouvet and Edwin F. Piscator amongst others.

Practically speaking, however, it is worth asking what exactly was going on in Spanish stage directing? Ramón María del Valle-Inclán, Adrià Gual, Gregorio Martínez Sierra, Federico García Lorca, Cipriano de Rivas Cherif, Salvador Bartolozzi, Eduardo Ugarte, Max Aub, Alejandro Casona, Ricardo Baroja, R. Martínez Romarate and Rafael Dieste were innovative directors of their own companies and can be considered the first 'metteurs' in Spain. Additionally, it should be pointed out that, during the Second Spanish Republic (1931–1939), the female contribution to contemporary theatre and its future direction[4]

---

[2] Dru Dougherty and María Francisca Vilches de Frutos, *La escena madrileña entre 1918 y 1926: Análisis y documentación* (Madrid: Fundamentos, 1990).

[3] *Paseo por el teatro catalán 1929/1985 (entre dos congresos)*, Cuadernos *El Público*, 4 (Madrid: Centro de Documentación Teatral, 1985).

[4] Pilar Nieva de la Paz, *Autoras dramáticas españolas entre 1918 y 1936* (Madrid: C.S.I.C., 1993).

was quite outstanding with Pura Maortua de Ucelay, Pilar de Valderrama, Carmen Monné, Margarita Xirgu[5] and María Teresa León.

The well-known author, Ramon María del Valle-Inclán[6] (1866–1936), was one of the first dramatic theorists in Spain at the beginning of the twentieth century. In 1899, together with Nobel Prizewinner Jacinto Benavente, he founded the Teatro Artístico Libre, a company similar to Stanislavsky's Moscow Art Theatre and Antoine's Théâtre Libre. He was also the director of his own company, an independent group called El Cántaro Roto (1926),[7] where Rivas Cherif, Salvador Bartolozzi, the well-known actresses Josefina Blanco (Valle-Inclán's wife) and Herminia Peñaranda (Jacinto Grau's wife) worked. Valle-Inclán upheld the concept of theatre as spectacle paying special attention to lighting and the use of music as well as the plastic effects of design. He used the mask in the manner of Craig and proposed stylized scenic ideas, which were later advocated by Meyerhold and Tairov. Valle-Inclán explored poetic language in the theatre, working within the form's theatrical limits. He considered cinematography the new theatre. As a European vanguardist he turned to children's theatre in search of inspiration. In his farces he used hyperbolic processing in themes and characters. In many articles Valle-Inclán touted the importance of scenography. 'All theatre is a plastic creation. Literature is of secondary importance', he wrote in 1929. Armed with this ideology he advocated scenic renovation and the need to have scenic rotation during the performance of classical theatre.[8]

In 1898 Adrià Gual[9] (1872–1943) created Teatre Intim, an independent company inspired by Paul Fort's Théâtre d'Art, Antoine's Théâtre Libre and Lugné-Poe's Théâtre de l'Oeuvre. From 1908 to 1910 he worked as the Artistic Director in Espectacles-Audicions Graner and the Nova Empresa de Teatre Català, a synthesis between the modern theatre and the commercial viewpoint. He took over the direction of the Escola Catalana d'Art Dramàtic (1913–1934) which performed his plays and a modern repertory of Catalonian theatre: Àngel Guimerà, Josep Pin i

[5] Domènec Guansè, *Margarida Xirgu* (Barcelona: Alcides, 1963) and Antonina Rodrigo, *Margarita Xirgu y su teatro* (Barcelona: Planeta, 1974).

[6] Sumner Greenfield, *Valle. Anatomía de un teatro problemático* (Madrid: Taurus, 1990) and Jean-Marie Lavaud, *El teatro en prosa de Valle-Inclán (1899–1914)* (Madrid: PPU, 1992).

[7] Jean-Marie Lavaud, 'El nuevo edificio del Círculo de Bellas Artes y El cántaro roto, de Valle-Inclán', *Segismundo*, 11, 1975, pp. 237–254 and Jesús Rubio Jiménez, 'Valle-Inclán y los teatros independientes de su tiempo', *Letras de Deusto*, 20, no. 48, 1990, pp. 49–71.

[8] Salvador Martínez Cuenca, 'En pro del arte dramático: Lo que debe ser el teatro español. Opinión de don Ramón María del Valle-Inclán', *El Imparcial*, 8 December 1929, p. 8.

[9] Hermann Bonnin, 'La primera concepció de la *posada en escena* moderna a Catalunya', *Serra d'Or*, May 1981, pp. 356–358; Enric Gallén, 'El teatre', in *Història de la literatura catalana*, VIII, eds Comas and Molas, Riquer (Barcelona, Ariel, 1986), pp. 379–481; and Carles Batlle i Jordà, *Adriá Gual, mitja vida de modernisme* (Barcelona, Diputació, 1992).

Soler, Joan Puig i Ferrater, Josep Pous i Pagès, Ignasi Iglesias, Santiago Rusiñol, and Pompeu Crehuet amongst others. Gual defended the modern concept of the stage director's role and introduced innovative repertoires, stressing an interdisciplinary concept of theatre, where musical and plastic elements were as expressive as the words. As a designer he followed the methods of Appia and Craig, whilst striving towards a 'popular theatre' inspired by traditional legends and songs. In conclusion, Gaul saw the future of the theatre in terms of a 'spectacle' rather than as a literary manifestation.

Ten years later Alejandro Miquis (pseud. for Anselmo González) founded the Teatro de Arte,[10] a gesture influenced by European Independent Theatre: Antoine, Stanislavsky and Otto Brahm evidently serving as models. They defended the artistic rather than the commercial concept of the theatre, and presented plays by 'moralistic' playwrights such as Shaw, Goncourt and Wilde. They tried to delve deeply into psychological and social theatre, incorporating the cinematographic resources of the smaller screen into their 'mise-en-scène'.

Gregorio Martínez Sierra (1881–1947) was one of the most important 'metteurs' during this period. He collaborated in the Benavente and Valle-Inclán joint venture, Teatro Artístico Libre. As well as a theatrical manager and author, he directed the Compañía de arte dramático Gregorio Martínez Sierra before going to Hollywood.[11] He was adamant about the hegemony of the director so that an actor could work unhindered. In an unedited letter to his wife, María de la O'Lejárraga, a well-known politician and the co-author of their plays, he remarked that: 'I am more convinced each day that under good direction no actor can be bad: average ones seem good and bad ones seem average.'[12]

Like Appia, he stressed the importance of light in creating a suggestive atmosphere. He was deeply interested in the importance of scenery and costume design, appointing Max Reinhardt's disciple Siegfried Burmann, and designers such as Salvador Bartolozzi, Manuel Fontanals, Rafael Pérez Barradas, Fernando Mignoni, Santiago Ontañón and Salvador Alarma, amongst others, to supervise these aspects of theatrical production. He worked together with the musician Manuel de Falla and the painter Néstor Martín on the production of *El amor brujo* (1915), an

---

[10] Dru Dougherty, 'Una iniciativa de reforma teatral: El grupo Teatro de Arte (1908–1911)', in *Homenaje a Alonso Zamora Vicente,* IV (Madrid: Castalia, 1995).

[11] *Gregorio Martínez Sierra, Un teatro de arte en España, 1917–1925* (Madrid: Ediciones La Esfinge, 1925); C. Reyero Hermosilla, *Gregorio Martínez Sierra y su Teatro de Arte* (Madrid: Fundación Juan March, 1980), and Julio Enrique Checa Puerta, 'Los teatros de Gregorio Martínez Sierra', in *El teatro en España entre la tradición y la vanguardia (1918–1939)*, pp. 121–126.

[12] My sincere thanks to Professor Julio Checa Puerta for this information.

example of the interdisciplinary concept of theatre. In his own play, *Triángulo* (*Triangle*) (1930), he broke the fourth wall convention between the stage and the public by suggesting that the audience recommend the best way to end the performance. One of his main interests involved bringing foreign, classical and contemporary Spanish texts to the stage in a fresh manner. He staged Federico García Lorca's *El maleficio de la mariposa* (*The Butterfly's Evil Spell*) (1920) in the Eslava Theatre.

'A play, is, above all, a good director',[13] said Federico García Lorca (1898–1936) in 1930. He created and led independent groups: the Teatro Cachiporra Andaluz (1923), La Barraca (1932) – one of the most interesting attempts to found a Spanish National Theatre – and Títeres de Cachiporra (1934). He also collaborated on occasion with other fringe groups such as Caracol (1928–1930) and Anfistora (1930).[14]

In the complex semiological process of theatre, Lorca supported having the director in the main role. He thought Romain Rolland's theories of the theatre reflected contemporary society, providing a space for the plays of young dramatists. With this idea in mind, he founded La Barraca, a collective company in which such important plastic artists as Benjamín Palencia, José Caballero and Santiago Ontañón collaborated. However, he was also interested in classic texts and, like Reinhardt, he insisted on contemporary versions of the classics. To Mildred Adams, in 1932, he explained his viewpoint on staging classic theatre in a modern way 'as new as the latest experiment and as old as the most ancient technique of stage setting and gesture'.[15] He was one of the first dramatists in Europe to revise classic texts, cutting out many roles and adding situational characters and songs so as to interest the general public. He was very proud of his production of Lope de Vega's *La dama boba* (*The Idiot Lady*) (1934), which ran for 200 performances in Argentina.[16]

For Federico García Lorca the 'metteur' created the knowledge which permitted a synthesis between traditionalists and vanguardists. In this sense, old theatre would be revived and be in tune with 'the rhythm of the era'. The director's work involved modernizing the text, and pointing out to the performers the intensity of their gestures, vocalization and

---

[13] Enrique Moreno Báez, 'La Barraca', in Andrés Soria Olmedo, *Treinta entrevistas a Federico García Lorca* (Madrid: Aguilar, 1988). See María Francisca Vilches de Frutos and Dru Dougherty, 'Federico García Lorca, director de escena', in *El teatro en España entre la tradición y la vanguardia (1918–1939)*, pp. 241–251.

[14] Federico García Lorca also directed for the commercial theatre with a number of prestigious companies of the time: Compañía Martínez Sierra, Compañía Díaz Artigas-Collado, Compañía Margarita Xirgu and Compañía Lola Membrives.

[15] Mildred Adams, 'The Theatre in the Spanish Republic', *Theatre Arts Monthly*, March 1932, in Federico García Lorca, *Obras completas* (Madrid: Aguilar, 1971), p. 1703

[16] Luis Sáenz de la Calzada, *'La Barraca' teatro universitario* (Madrid: Revista de Occidente, 1976), p. 54.

characterization; producing a stylized design using light to suggest space, feelings and situations, and selecting the appropriate music with the emphasis placed on the plastic nature of theatrical fashion. He was one of the first to adequately express theatrical rhythm and the importance of tone. Margarita Ucelay, the director of Anfistora, pointed out Federico García Lorca's particular interest in the symphonic use of voices, music, choreographic rhythm and the suggestion of colours in the costume design.[17] Lorca thought all of these scenic languages were an instrument at the disposal of the 'metteur'. In his productions he worked as a designer, figurist, composer and choreographer. When he developed La Barraca with Eduardo Ugarte he wrote: 'I choose, adapt, and direct the scenography and interpretation; I compose the music and dance.'[18]

Lorca broke down the wall between dramatic fiction and reality by introducing the author himself as a character. He advised Mildred Adams that in a stylized 'mise-en-scène', the 'plays of today, acted in the modern manner, very simply explained ahead of time and presented with extreme simplicity, are necessary for the success of our plan which makes experimental theatre so interesting'. To this he added his idea of performing the same play in two different ways on two consecutive days: 'the first one in an old fashioned and realistic way; the second in a simple and stylized way.' With his group Títeres de Cachiporra (1934) he revived the traditional puppet theatre in order to delve into stylized forms of expression; a way of exploring through expressionism.

In his personal writing, currently preserved by his family, Lorca was adamant about the importance of the actor. He saw the voice and physical appearance as being very useful. He wrote:

Women –
Carmen Tellez – Jovellanos 7 –
Fine voice. Dramatic – Good Spanish – Passionate
Reads well. Sense of prose – No poetic sense
                    Role of peasant woman.

---

[17] Margarita Ucelay, 'Federico García Lorca y el Club Teatral Anfistora: el dramaturgo como director de escena', in *Lecciones sobre Federico García Lorca*, ed. Andrés Soria Olmedo (Granada: Comisión Nacional del Cincuentenario, 1986), pp. 51–64, and 'El Club Teatral Anfistora', in *El teatro en España entre la tradición y la vanguardia (1918–1939)*, pp. 453–467.

[18] Silvio d'Amico, 'Encuentro con Federico García Lorca', *Il Dramma*, Turín, 15 May 1946, translated by Andrés Soria Olmedo, *Treinta entrevistas a Federico García Lorca*, p. 203. In 1934 he told Juan Chabás: 'Fatigue, but pleasurable. And besides after the rehearsals and experiences I feel that I'm becoming a stage director, a difficult and slow training.' (Federico García Lorca, *Obras completas*, p. 175).

The beginning of the 1920s were influenced by the theoretical and practical work of Cipriano de Rivas Cherif (1891–1967).[19] After living in Italy, where he studied Craig's theories, and travelling through France, acquiring invaluable theatrical experience, he cooperated in the Teatro de la Escuela Nueva (1919–1921), trying to create a massive theatre with the same type of open-air performances staged by Max Reinhardt, and to encourage the cooperation of performers and authors. He directed Carmen Monné and Ricardo Baroja's Mirlo Blanco (1926–1927), an art theatre group,[20] and founded Caracol (1928) in his own Rex Theatre.[21] After work as a literary advisor in Irene López de Heredia's Company (1929) he took over the directorship of the Teatro Español, founded the Compañía Clásica de Arte Moderno (1930) and started his long-lasting collaboration with the well-known actress Margarita Xirgu. Together they received huge critical acclaim for a series of productions beginning with Seneca's *Medea* staged in 1933, which was followed by Valle-Inclán's *Divinas palabras* (*Divine Words*) (1933), Calderón's *El alcalde de Zalamea* (*The Mayor of Zalamea*) (1934), Lorca's *Yerma* (1935) and Lope de Vega's *Fuenteovejuna* performed in an open-air theatre in the Max Reinhardt style in 1935. Rivas Cherif also directed the National Lyric Theatre (1932), the Compañía Nacional de Arte Moderno (1932) and the Estudio de Arte Dramático del Teatro Español (1933). At the end of 1933, the government granted him the Teatro María Guerrero where he founded the cooperative Teatro Escuela de Arte in the manner of Gémier and Brahm. As a prisoner in the Dueso Prison after the Civil War, he founded the Teatro Escuela del Penal del Dueso.

Rivas Cherif published many newspaper articles about the 'metteur',[22] which defended the theatre as a visual rather than literary form. In a letter written to the Madrid Town Council he wrote:

---

[19] Manuel Tuñón de Lara, *Medio siglo de cultura española* (*1855–1936*) (Madrid: Tecnos, 1977), pp. 163–182. See also the articles by Juan Aguilera Sastre, Manuel Aznar Soler and Enrique de Rivas in *Cipriano de Rivas Cherif. Retrato de una utopía*, Cuadernos *El Público*, 42, (Madrid: Centro de Documentación Teatral, 1989).

[20] For the first time The Mirlo Blanco offered plays by Spanish vanguardist authors: Valle-Inclán, Pío and Ricardo Baroja, Claudio de la Torre, Edgar Neville and Beatriz Galindo (pseud. of Isabel Oyorzábal de Palencia) among others. In the performance of *Los cuernos de don Friolera* by Valle-Inclán he was the puppet's voice. See Juan Aguilera Sastre, 'La labor renovadora de Cipriano Rivas Cherif en el teatro español: El Mirlo Blanco y El Cántaro Roto', *Segismundo*, nos. 39–40, 1984, pp. 233–245.

[21] Magda Donato (pseud. For Carmen Nelken), Felipe Llunch Garín and the set designer Salvador Bartolozzi collaborated in this experimental theatre. They earned great critical success with Jean Cocteau's *Orfeo*, Federico García Lorca's *La zapatera prodigiosa* and *Un sueño de la razón*, an interesting play about lesbian love which he wrote and which was performed in the modern manner.

[22] *Cómo hacer teatro: Apuntes de orientación profesional en las artes y oficios del teatro español*, ed. Enrique de Rivas (Valencia: Pre-textos, 1991) sum up his theatrical theories.

I, on the other hand, believe that theatre preferably requires the greatest directive unity possible, despite the unavoidable division of labour according to each person's role. In effect, the modern tendency in the world's first theatres grants the director absolute powers, albeit to the disadvantage of the author, which in my opinion is excessive but which tends to specialize the playwright's literary work in truly theatrical fashion; i.e. with a view to representing and not reading.[23]

In fact, Rivas Cherif raised many points with regard to the director and theatre practice: the need to increase the 'metteur's' protagonism; the latter's importance in world theatre, as well as taking into account the complexity of the genre as another element. Rivas Cherif was one of the first to write about the dramatist's role and to quote Tairov's theories. He upheld the capacity of the stage director to introduce changes to classic texts and to coordinate the designer's work. In his production of Calderón's *El gran teatro del mundo* (*The Great Theatre of the World*) (1930), he worked with the plastic artist Burmann, whose scenic design operated on different levels, these being occupied by the characters according to their status and being accentuated by the nuances of lighting. Rivas Cherif, also upholding Stanislavsky's viewpoint regarding the pedagogical function of the theatre for the people as a whole, was one of the most important defenders of a National Theatre. He fought for the creation of the National Theatre School Foundation in order to train good professionals.

Yet, there were other experiments in the art of 'mise en scène'. The plastic enterprises of Salvador Bartolozzi and his Teatro Pinocho, a stimulating experiment which utilized both light to create psychological atmosphere and the expressive nature of the puppet theatre, should not be forgotten. During the period Rafael Martínez Romarate and Pilar de Valderrama founded Fantasio (1929) in their own home; an example of the Chamber Theatre where they insisted on using lighting and the plastic effect of colours in costumes and scenic design. In the commercial theatre, Enrique Rambal and Ramón Caralt introduced spectacular re-runs of the North American police melodrama to Spain. They were absorbed in the application of cinematographic techniques, the separation of pit and scenery, the use of light, and the inclusion of brief and rapid scenes.

Romain Rolland's theories regarding the theatre's social function found a loyal following in an experiment by the University Theatre of Valencia, El Búho (1933–1936), created by Lluís Llana and Eduardo Muñoz. This company rejected the commercial bourgeois theatre and

---

[23] Cipriano de Rivas Cherif, 'La concesión del teatro español: Una carta del asesor literario de Margarita Xirgu a los concejales firmantes de la ponencia municipal, *Heraldo de Madrid*, 25 February 1931, p. 6.

worked towards a synthetic 'mise-en-scène' using multifunctional designs which allowed them to tour small Spanish towns. They performed classical Spanish theatre in a more contemporary style. At the time of the Civil War, El Búho started a second period directed at first by the playwright Max Aub (1903–72), a defender of the National Theatre, and afterwards by Manuel Romeu and Francisco Canet. They upheld Craig's theories and performed anti-fascist plays by Rafael Alberti, Max Aub and Valle-Inclán.[24]

Similarly, the Government created Misiones Pedagógicas in 1931, another attempt to bring theatre and culture to rural areas.[25] Directed by Rafael Marquina and Alejandro Casona (1905–1965) they performed classic theatre in the open air with a naive stylized design, placing enormous importance upon the rhythm of music and verse. After 1933 they worked in the Puppet Theatre under the direction of Rafael Dieste.

Many young playwrights were also tempted to direct for the stage. In an interview given to the newspaper *Heraldo de Madrid*, a famous author, twenty years after José López Rubio before him, professed a passion for directing:

Do you know what I would love to do? I would love to manage a theatre. This is a job unknown to Spain. Apart from Martínez Sierra, theatres here need literary animation in the European style, i.e. a man in first place, but a man who is not a business man or an author or the main actor. It is a matter of adaptation, of harmonization. Like in the cinema. Like cinema directors.[26]

Rolland's theories are clearly discernible in the agit-prop groups created during the Civil War (1936–1939): García Lorca, Las Guerrillas del Teatro and Grupo de Teatro Popular de Madrid are amongst the best known.[27] But María Teresa León's groups were also well-known: Nueva Escena (1936) in which plastic artists such as Fontanals, Ontañón, Prieto, Sancha and Gaya collaborated; Teatro de Arte y Propaganda (1937) which produced the successful performance of Cervantes' *Numancia* and the Cine-Teatro Club de la Alianza de Intelectuales Antifascistas (1938).

---

[24] Manuel Aznar Soler, 'El Búho: Teatro de la F.U.E. de la Universidad de Valencia', in *El teatro en España entre la tradición y la vanguardia (1918–1939)* pp. 415–427.

[25] Eugenio Otero Urtaza, *Las Misiones Pedagógicas: Una experiencia de educación popular* (A Coruña: Ediciós do Castro, 1982). See also Gloria Rey Faraldos, 'El teatro de las Misiones Pedagógicas' and Juan María Díez Taboada, 'Alejandro Casona en su primera época' in *El teatro en España entre la tradición y la vanguardia (1918–1939)*, pp. 153–164 and 111–119.

[26] José Luis Salado, 'Los nuevos: José López Rubio, o el hombre que llena de piedras sus bolsillos', *Heraldo de Madrid*, 10 April 1930, p. 8.

[27] Robert Marrast, *El teatre durant la guerra civil espanyola. Assaig d'historia y documents* (Barcelona: Institut del Teatre de Barcelona, 1978).

The Spanish Post-Civil War Period (1939–1975)

After the Civil War, the commercial theatre really took over. Only a few examples of the innovative period survived: some independent groups, some directors in national theatres and the creation of the National Chamber Theatre.

As well as Rivas Cherif's group created in the Dueso Prison, there were other directors leading independent groups:[28] José Luis Alonso, Carmen Troitiño, Alfonso Sastre,[29] José María de Quinto, José Gordon, Antonio de Cabo, Rafael Richard, Juan Germán Schroeder, Marta Grau, Arturo Carbonell, Modesto Higueras, Esteve Polls, José María Loperena, Antonio Chic and Gustavo Pérez Puig, amongst others. The most important groups were: Teatro de Arte (1941), Teatro de Estudio (1942), Arte Nuevo (1946), Teatro Universitario de Ensayo (1947), La Vaca Flaca (1948), La Carátula (1949), Teatro de Cámara de Barcelona (1949), Teatro Yorick (1949), Teatro Experimental de Barcelona (1950), Teatro Español Universitario (1952), Teatro de Cámara de Madrid (1952), Teatro de Hoy (1953) and Agrupación de Teatro Experimental (1953).

These groups supported the social and political function of theatre, rejecting the existing attitude in Spain. They embraced the North American realistic playwrights: O'Neill, Thornton Wilder, Arthur Miller and Tennessee Williams; the French existentialists and the 'classics' which could be staged in the open-air. They presented plays written by 'dangerous' or contentious Spanish playwrights such as Azorín, Joan Brossa, Antonio Buero Vallejo and Alfonso Sastre. They worked with Craig, Reinhardt and Brecht's epic theatre techniques: embracing small scenes, the use of a narrator's voice, the fragmentary mixture of past and present, cinematic methods, and the introduction of the author himself as a character. Only a few groups, however, performed in the national theatres.

At the same time Felipe Lluch, Luis Escobar, Humberto Pérez de la Ossa, Claudio de la Torre and Cayetano Luca de Tena directed plays for the Government's national theatres: the María Guerrero and the Español.[30] Whilst the conservative government was in power, the critics

---

[28] José Ramón Fernández, 'Teatro de búsqueda: Las representaciones de Cámara y Ensayo en los teatros oficiales (1939–1960)' in *Historia de los teatros nacionales*, I (1939–1962), ed. Andrés Peláez (Madrid: Centro de Documentación Teatral, 1993), pp. 133–141.
[29] In 1950 he wrote the *Manifesto of Theatre for Social Agitation* (*Manifiesto de agitación política*), an important contribution to theatrical theories in Spain and in 1960 he founded another group: Grupo de Teatro Realista. See *Alfonso Sastre. Noticia de una ausencia*, Cuadernos *El Público*, no. 38 (Madrid: Centro de Documentación Teatral, 1988).
[30] See the articles by Juan Aguilera, Lola Santa-Cruz, Felipe Higuera, Julio Checa, Pilar Nieva and José Ramón Fernández in *Historia de los teatros nacionales*, I, ed. Andrés Peláez.

and the public were supporters of the 'metteur's' importance and the concepts of the National Theatre. They tried to create a 'mise-en-scène' with classical texts, taking special care over design, choreography and music. From the beginning, under Felipe Lluch's direction, plastic artists such as Salvador Dalí, Siegfried Burmann, José Caballero, Emilio Burgos and Víctor María Cortezo, and musicians such as Ernst Halffter, Joaquín Rodrigo, Manuel Parada and Fernando Moraleda worked for the national theatres, with Rafael Martínez Romarate being responsible for lighting. They brought plays such as Jean Giradoux's *Electra* (1942); J.B. Prestley's *Time and the Conways* (1942) and *Music at Night* (1953); Thornton Wilder's *Our Town* (1944); Jean Paul Sartre's *Huis-clos* (1947); Jean Anouilh's *Medea* (1952), and Tennessee Williams' *Summer and Smoke* (1952) to Spain. Dalí's design for José Zorrilla's *Don Juan Tenorio* (1949) was acclaimed as a huge success.

We should not forget Felipe Lluch's (1906–1941) impact as a disciple of Cipriano de Rivas Cherif (Caracol and Teatro de Escuela de Arte) and María Teresa León (Teatro de Arte y Propaganda). Whilst fighting for the creation of the National Theatre he defended the need to increase the 'metteur's' protagonism, the capacity of the stage director to introduce changes in classic texts and to coordinate the designer's work, and the need to promote the pedagogical function of theatre for the people. In 1940 he founded the first national theatre at the Teatro Español. Cayetano Luca de Tena (1917), a disciple of Lluch, followed him as the leader of the national Teatro Español between 1942–1952 where Buero Vallejo's *Historia de una escalera* (*Story of a Staircase*) (1949) was performed, and which was the first theatre to use scenic gyration in Calderón's *La dama duende* (*The Phantom Lady*) (1942). Luis Escobar together with Huberto Pérez de la Ossa and Claudio de la Torre led the Teatro Nacional María Guerrero. Escobar was also well-known for the direction of an important Spanish play, Buero Vallejo's *En la ardiente oscuridad* (*In the Burning Darkness*) (1950), and was the first to direct García Lorca's play *Yerma* (1960) after the Civil War.

The signing of the Marshall Plan exposed Spain to a new political view-point which culminated in 1975 with Franco's death. In 1954 the Government created the Teatro Nacional de Cámara y Ensayo (National Chamber Theatre), sponsored with public donations and directed by Modesto Higueras who had collaborated with Federico García Lorca in La Barraca.[31] José Luis Alonso and Carmen Troitiño's Teatro de Cámara de Madrid provided Higueras with an obvious model. It is here that we may find the main Spanish directors of this time: José Luis Alonso,

---

[31] At the same time the Real Escuela Superior de Arte Dramático (Royal Higher School for Dramatic Arts) was created.

Miguel Narros, Adolfo Marsillach and Ricard Salvat, amongst others. Formed in chamber groups and well-versed in many languages and cultures they attempted to introduce the most important European plays to Spain. Shortly after its first performance, the spectators of the Teatro Nacional de Cámara y Ensayo could see many of the most important plays of the North American naturalist dramatists, epic theatre, the Theatre of Cruelty, existentialist theatre, Germanic expressionism, the Theatre of the Absurd and the Living Theatre. Meanwhile José Tamayo led the national Teatro Español from 1954 to 1962 as did Claudio de la Torre the Teatro María Guerrero from 1954 to 1960.

Jose Tamayo (1928),[32] educated in the University Theatre (Teatro Universitario Lope de Vega), founded the Lope de Vega Company. The success of his production of Arthur Miller's *Death of a Salesman* (1952) secured him appointment as director of the Teatro Español. From 1961 onwards he directed his own company in the Teatro Bellas Artes where he collaborated with well-known international plastic artists such as Benjamín Palencia, Daniel Vázquez Díaz, José Caballero and Siegfried Burmann, and musicians such as Joaquín Rodrigo, Cristóbal and Ernst Halffter. He directed large-scale musicals including the well-known *Antología de la Zarzuela* (1966). For the first time after the Civil War he performed three Valle-Inclán pieces, *Divinas palabras* (*Divine Words*) (1961); *Luces de bohemia* (*Bohemian Lights*) (1971) and *Tirano Banderas* (1974); and Garciá Lorca's *Bodas de sangre* (*Blood Wedding*) (1962). He researched the importance of large-scale shows according to the theories of Max Reinhardt and introduced the North American naturalist playwrights (Thornton Wilder, Miller, and Faulkner) to Spain, together with Brecht's epic theatre and the German expressionist dramatists Frisch and Dürrenmatt. His greatest successes included *Death of a Salesman* by Arthur Miller (1952); *Enrico IV* by Pirandello (1958); *La Orestiada* by Aeschylus (1959); *The Visit* by Dürrenmatt (1959); *Mother Courage and her Children* by Brecht (1966); *The Great Wall of China* by Max Frisch (1969) and *The Threepenny Opera* by Brecht (1979). He also directed plays written by French playwrights such as Jean Anouilh, Albert Camus and Jean Cocteau.

Jose Luis Alonso (1924–1992)[33] was also schooled in the chamber theatre from 1948 (Teatro de la Independencia, El Duende and Teatro de Cámara de Madrid) and took over the management of the Teatro Nacional María Guerrero in 1961. He directed important plays from the French theatre: Anouilh, Claudel, Cocteau, Giradoux and Sartre, and two

[32] Andrés Peláez, ed., *50 años de teatro. José Tamayo (1941–1951)*, (Madrid: Centro de Documentación Teatral 1991).
[33] Juan Antonio Hormigón, ed., *Teatro de cada día de José Luis Alonso* (Madrid: Ministerio de Cultura, 1991).

years after the first performance of Ionesco's *Rhinoceros* (1961) he intro-
duced it to Spain. He had great success with the plays of O'Neill,
Pirandello and Williams; the epic theatre with *The Caucasian Chalk Circle*
(1971) and the Russian naturalist theatre: Chekhov, Gorky and Turgenev.
He was very interested in Spanish classical drama, especially the works
of Calderón de la Barca, Lope de Vega and Tirso de Molina; Pérez
Galdós and the historical Spanish vanguards García Lorca, Valle-Inclán,
Alberti and Unamuno; the Spanish pre-war theatre: Benavente and
Arniches; the Spanish humourous theatre: Jardiel Poncela and Mihura;
and contemporary Spanish playwrights such as Francisco Nieva, Antonio Gala, Alfredo Mañas and Domingo Miras. Great critical success came
with *Eloísa está debajo de un almendro* (*Eloise is Under an Almond Tree*)
by Jardiel Poncela (1961); *The Mad Woman of Chaillot* by Giraudoux
(1962); *Los caciques* (*The Local Rulers*) by Arniches (1962); *La dama duende*
(*The Phantom Lady*) by Calderón, presented in New York (1965); *Romance
de lobos* (*Ballad of Wolves*) by Valle-Inclán (1970); *Misericordia* by Pérez
Galdós (1972); *The Glass Menagerie* (1978) and *Cat on a Hot Tin Roof* by
Williams (1979); *La enamorada del rey* (*The Girl who loved the King*) by
Valle-Inclán and García Lorca's *El retablillo de don Cristóbal* (The 're-
tabillo' of Don Cristobal) (1988), and *El alcalde de Zalamea* (*The Mayor of
Zalamea*) by Calderón (1988). It is worth remembering the acclaim of the
Antonio Gala plays he directed. José Luis Alonso took special care with
actors' performances, the movement of groups and the plastic effects of
design in scenery and costumes.

Miguel Narros, also a designer and an actor, was a disciple of Jean
Vilar at the TNP (Theatre National Popular) in Paris. He worked in the
university and chamber theatre (Teatro Popular Universitario, Pequeño
Teatro de Barcelona, Dido Pequeño Teatro de Madrid, Teatro Estable de
Madrid, Teatro Estable Castellano and Teatro de Arte) and was Artistic
Director of the Teatro Español in Madrid from 1966 to 1971 and from
1984 to 1990. His main interest has lain in bringing to the stage foreign
and Spanish classical texts in a sharp contemporary style: Aristophanes,
Cervantes, Lope de Vega, Shakespeare, Tirso de Molina, Guillén de
Castro, Molière and Moratín have been reworked in collaboration with
plastic artists such as Francisco Nieva, Pablo Gago, Fabià Puigserver,
Vitín Cortezo, Siegfried Burmann and Andrea d'Odorico. He worked
with texts by Chekhov, Strindberg, O'Neill and Pirandello, and introduced to Spain important plays by Beckett, Sartre, Dürrenmatt, Wesker,
Anouilh, Delaney and Koltès. He directed Spanish pre-Civil War play-
wrights such as Benavente, García Lorca and Valle-Inclán; and the con-
temporary playwrights Fernando Arrabal, Manuel Pombo, Buero Vallejo,
Diego Salvador, Luis Riaza, Alfonso Vallejo, Antonio Gala, Jaime Salom,
Ignacio Amestoy and Vargas Llosa. He found critical success in *The
Affected Ladies* by Molière (1967); *Así que pasen cinco años* (*When Five Years*

Pass) by García Lorca (1978); *Six Characters in Search of an Author* by Pirandello (1982); *Endgame* by Beckett (1984); *El castigo sin venganza* (*The Wise Man's Punishment*) by Lope de Vega (1985); *A Midsummer Night's Dream* by Shakespeare (1986), and *La malquerida* (*The Unloved*) by Benavente (1987). Additionally he fought for the creation of a theatre school where future generations of professionals could be properly trained.

Adolfo Marsillach (1928), also an actor, is well-known for the many productions in Spain which followed after his première of Peter Weiss's *Marat-Sade* and a production of Molière's *Tartuffe* (1969). Influenced by Artaud's ideas, he no longer thought of theatre as just entertainment but as action with 'total' realism. He took great care with the sound of voices, songs and music, dancing and movement in general; he used gloomy lighting and the work of the actor to transmit violence, sexuality and the breaking of social taboos, all taking place beyond the confines of the stage. After Franco's death he took over the artistic directorship of the Compañía Nacional de Teatro Clásico (National Company of Classical Theatre) where he still works today.

Ricard Salvat (1934), educated in university theatre (Teatre Viu and Dido Pequeño Teatro), was one of the main defenders of the Catalonian National Theatre and epic theatre, editing directly from German to Catalan. In 1960, together with Maria Aurèlia Capmany, he founded the Escola d'Art Dramàtic Adrià Gual, one of the most important Spanish theatres of the 1960s. In this school he taught Stanislavsky's Method Acting, Piscator and Brecht's theories, and practices of alienation and distancing. He was meticulous in his designs, trying to rupture the concept of the fourth wall. He introduced plays by Goethe, Brecht, Sartre, Pirandello and many important contemporary playwrights to Spain, especially Franz Xaver Kroetz and Peter Handke. Salvat was highly successful with *Primera història d'Esther* (*The First Story of Esther*) and *Ronda de mort a Sinera* (*Dance of Death of Sinera*) (1966), both by Salvador Espriu. In 1971 he took over the management of Barcelona's National Theatre, named after the Companya Àngel Guimerà.

During these years, many university and independent groups[34] who identified with total theatre sprang up searching for a 'popular concept' over and above that of the commercial theatre. They agreed with Roger Planchon that 'scenic writing' should express the importance of the director's work. Many of these groups performed plays in the Teatro Nacional de Cámara y Ensayo and had tremendous success with plays

---

[34] María Francisca Vilches de Frutos, 'El Teatro Nacional de Cámara y Ensayo. Auge de los grupos de teatro independiente (1960–1975)', in *Historia de los teatros nacionales (1975–1994)*, II, ed. Andrés Peláez (Madrid: Centro de Documentación Teatral, 1995).

such as Espriu's *Ronda de mort a Sinera* (1966); Dürrenmatt's *Proceso de la sombra de los burros* (1966); *Espectáculos cátaros '67* (*Cátaros's collective creation*) (1967); *Striptease* and *Out at Sea* by Mrozek (1967); Weiss's *Marat-Sade* (1968); Boadella's *El diario* (*The Diary*) (1969) and Tábano's *Castañuela 70* (*Castanet 70*) (1970). All of these works collectively used vaudeville and cabaret techniques, as well as parody to transform themes, myths, genres, and styles, just like the Living Theatre. Some of these directors went on, after 1975, to become outstanding figures in Spanish theatre: Frederic Roda (Agrupació Dramatica de Barcelona, 1955); José Gordón, Miguel Narros, José María de Quinto and Ricard Salvat (Dido Pequeño Teatro, 1960); Maria Aurèlia Capmany and Ricard Salvat (Escola d'Art Dramàtic Adrià Gual, 1960); Albert Boadella, Carlota Soldevilla and Antón Font (Els Joglars, 1962); María López, Miguel Narros, José Carlos Plaza and William Layton (Teatro Estudio de Madrid, 1963); Gonzalo Pérez de Olaguer (Bambalinas, 1963); Santiago Sans, Mario Gas and Joan Manuel Gisbert (Gogo, 1963); Angel Facio, Miguel Arrieta and Fermín Cabal (Los Goliardos, 1964); Josep Montanyès and Josep Maria Segarra (Grup d'Estudis Teatrals d'Horta, 1964); Manuel Serra, Francesc Nel.lo, Ventura Pons, Feliu Formosa, Mario Gas, Fabià Puigserver, Alfred Lucchetti and Carlota Soldevilla (Grup de Teatre Independent, 1966); Layton, Plaza and Pedro Carvajal (Teatro Experimental Independiente, 1968); Joan Baixas (La Claca, 1968); Santiago Sans (Jocs a la Sorra, 1968); Hermann Bonninn (Teatre Experimental del Institut del Teatre de Barcelona, 1970); Alberto Miralles (Cátaro, 1968); Lluís Pasqual (La Tartana); José Luis Alonso de Santos, Fermín Cabal, Guillermo Heras and Juan Margallo (Tábano, 1968); Joan Font (Comediants, 1972); Josep Anton Codina (Grup de l'Escola de Teatre de l'Orfeó de Sants, 1973), and Joan Ollé (Dagoll-Dagom, 1974).

Since the 1960s the knowledge imparted by the main theoretical essayists on directing for the stage has made its way into Spain's dramaturgy as the country's directors analyzed and tried to put into practice the principal theoretical facets of Artaud, Brecht, Craig, Grotowski, Komissarzhevsky, the Living Theatre, Meyerhold, Piscator, Planchon, Reinhardt, Stanislavsky and Jean Vilar. Many productions drew on the alienating and distancing techniques of Reinhardt, Piscator and Brecht. Directors worked with Artaud's Theatre of Cruelty, and some performances appeared to be the consequence of improvisational research as advocated by Grotowski's Laboratory Theatre. The post 1960 directors liked the emotional impact of Brecht's visual search for a marriage between political and aesthetic radicalism seeking an anti-realistic style. Many professionals were interested in Pirandello's theatrical schemes and in Komissarzhevsky's synthesis theatre. As with Jean Vilar, they insisted that the theatre should be available to everyone, acting as a public service.

The main characteristic of these collective groups was probably the rejection of dramatic texts as something definite and unchangeable. They supported the theatrical re-transformation of non-dramatic texts and worked with resources from parody and farce. They also came up with documentary theatre from newspaper texts, and defended the value of an actor's improvisation from a concrete situation applying the techniques of 'amplification' and 'elipsis'. They delved into the connotative capacity of gesture, mimic and tonal variations, the use of masks; choreographic movements; the plastic potential of design and costumes; the psychological possibilities of music, and the emphasis on dramatic action to touch on situations. Els Joglars, a company of importance, believed that mime was 'experimental art par excellence'.[35] They worked on 'happening' performances, street shows, scenic carnival practices, open air productions using masks, stilts, puppets and the use of fire. Comediants triumphed in the 1980s and 1990s.

Nevertheless, at the head of a concept of theatre as spectacle came a defence by many groups of the main elements of drama. The actors came first in a unipersonal performance with synthetic design and an important use of the possibilities of light. They embraced theatre as the result of an actor's discipline, but, nevertheless, they chose their own conditions which had a great influence on the choice of multifunctional, symbolic and inexpensive scenographies. Regarding the production of *Quejío* by Salvador Távora, the manager of La Cuadra, Javier Rodríguez Piñero stated:

The main outstanding scenic point in *Quejío* is, or was, a drum filled with stones, paving stones, or a similar load, together with some ropes which anchored the men to the drum.[36]

They performed texts from the Theatre of Cruelty: Artaud, Jarry, Genet and Virgilio Piñera; the French existentialist Sartre; the Theatre of the Absurd: Beckett, Adamov, Ionesco, Obey and Vian; the German expressionists, combining irony and the grotesque: Dürrenmatt, Max Frisch, Peter Handke and Tankred Dorst; Brecht's epic theatre; English and North American texts, the psychological drama of O'Neill, and the humorous absurdism of Edward Albee, William Inge, Arthur Miller, Tennessee Williams, Shelagh Delaney, Harold Pinter and John Osborne; and South American social realist dramas. They were deeply interested in social and expressionist works of the 'Generación silenciada' (The

---

[35] See the hand-out programme of *El diario* preserved in the Centro de Documentación Teatral in Madrid.
[36] Javier Rodríguez Piñero, 'La saga de las máquinas y la llegada de los animales', in *La Cuadra en olor de Alhucema*, Cuadernos *El Público* (Madrid: Centro de Documentación Teatral, 1988).

Silenced Generation): Juan Antonio Castro, Ángel García Pintado, Jerónimo López Mozos, José Martín Elizondo, Fernando Martín Iniesta, Antonio Martínez Ballesteros, Manuel Martínez Mediero, Luis Matilla, Alberto Miralles, Lauro Olmo, Luis Riaza, José María Rodríguez Méndez, Miguel Romeo Esteo and José Ruibal. In Catalonia they worked with Catalonian experimental dramas by Joan Brossa, Manuel Pedrolo, Salvador Espriu, Maria Aurèlia Capmany, Josep Maria Muñoz i Pujol, Benet i Jornet and Jordi Teixidor. Beckett, Frisch, Ionesco, O'Neill, Pirandello, Pinget, Pinter and Williams were the favoured playwrights. They started to re-use the historic vanguardists: Valle-Inclán, García Lorca, Alberti, Max Aub and Jacinto Grau. Amongst the classics they chose Shakespeare, Molière, Guelderode, Büchner, Strindberg, Chekhov and Shaw.

The Democratic Period (1975–1995)

After Franco's death (1975) the transition towards a complete democracy in Spain began. On April 1st 1978, the censorship laws were repealed and the Law of Freedom of Speech was introduced. In 1985 the Instituto de las Artes Escénicas y de la Música (National Institute for Performing Arts and Music I.N.A.E.M.) was created, with four theatrical organizations: Centro Dramático Nacional (The National Drama Centre), directed in turn by Adolfo Marsillach, Núria Espert, José Luis Gómez, Ramón Tamayo, Lluís Pasqual and José Carlos Plaza; the Centro Nacional de Nuevas Tendencias Escénicas (The National Centre for New Stage Trends), directed by Guillermo Heras (1984); the Compañía Nacional de Teatro Clásico (The Classic Theatre Company) directed by Adolfo Marsillach and Rafael Pérez Sierra (1985), and the Teatro Nacional Lírico de la Zarzuela (The Zarzuela Lyrical National Theatre), directed initially by José Luis Alonso. The I.N.A.E.M.'s main functions were to protect and promote theatrical activities in Spain and to open up many new possibilities for cooperation between theatrical professionals and public institutions. In 1993 the I.N.A.E.M. created the Red Nacional de Teatros y Auditorios (National Network of Theatres and Auditoria), an important attempt to offer public theatres to companies. At the same time, Spain itself was politically reorganized into Comunidades Autónomas (Autonomous Communities). Centres for the production and study of theatre were also established at these new government levels. Some of the seventeen autonomous communities have their own regional drama centres, as well as their own theatre companies and festivals.[37]

---

[37] María Francisca Vilches de Frutos, *Spain* in *The World Encyclopedia of Contemporary Theatre*, ed. Don Rubin (London and New York: Routledge, 1994), pp. 790–804.

'Metteurs' formed in the chamber companies and independent groups became artistic directors of the public theatres which developed after the P.S.O.E.'s (Socialist Party) arrival to power, these being Hermann Bonninn, Manuel Canseco, Mario Gas, Guillermo Heras, Juan Margallo, Josep Montanyès, Miguel Narros, César Oliva, Lluís Pasqual, José Carlos Plaza, José Sanchis Sinisterra and Rodolf Sirera. Other directors were able to perform their plays in public places: Angel Alonso, Albert Boadella, Antonio Corencia, Angel Facio, Enric Flores, Josep Maria Flotats, Joan Font, Feliu Formosa, Ariel García Valdés, José Luis Gómez, Ángel González Vergel, Ángel Gutiérrez, Emilio Hernández, Juan Antonio Hormigón, Antonio Malonda, Jordi Mesalles, Alberto Miralles, Pilar Miró, Josefina Molina, Francesc Nel.lo, Pere Planella, Carmen Portacelli, Fabià Puigserver, Juan Antonio Quintana, María Ruiz, Santiago Sans and Carles Santos. The public theatre network also incorporated into their repertoires the work of a new generation of young playwrights: Sergi Belbel, Calixto Bieito, Ernesto Caballero, Amaya Curieses, Rodrigo García, Antonio Llopis, Sara Molina, Ignacio del Moral, Juan Carlos Pérez de la Fuente, Helena Pimienta, Antoni Tordera, Etelvino Vázquez and Alfonso Zurro, amongst others.

Many productions by the most important foreign stage directors came to Spain. The public theatre brought in performances directed by Peter Brook, Jean Vilar, Ariane Mnouchkine, Robert Wilson, Tadeusz Kantor, Heiner Müller, Pina Bausch, Dario Fo, Ingmar Bergman, Peter Stein, Giorgio Strehler, Antoine Vitez and Víctor García. At international festivals Spanish audiences were able to see the latest performances directed by the main European and American companies: the Comédie Française, the Royal National Theatre, the Royal Shakespeare Company, the Berlin Schaubühne, the Théâtre National Populaire and the Théâtre du Soleil, amongst others.

Their formation as independent groups has had an important influence on the theatrical language of public theatre in Spain. These relationships explain the important presence of images in large theatres. Emphasizing the visual elements rather than the text, they translated their own style to the main theatre. Audiences in the 1990s, even those who had proved most conservative, have come to accept some of the complex semiotic codes used by this theatrical style. Some different examples of this style were seen in the production of Pier Paolo Pasolini's *Calderón* (1988), directed by Guillermo Heras (a complex interpretation of the Spanish character achieved almost exclusively through visual images) and *Azaña, una pasión española* (*Azaña, a Spanish Passion*) (1988), based on the life and writings of Manuel Azaña, President of the Spanish Republic, which was directed by José Luis Gómez on an empty stage with extensive lighting which was deeply suggestive. Creations by some old groups such as Els Joglars, Comediants,

Dagoll-Dagom and La Cuadra, and by new groups such as La Fura del Baus, Vol.Ras and El Tricicle proved successful abroad in the 1990s.

The large public theatres gave official support to the productions of the historic Spanish vanguardists: Valle-Inclán, García Lorca, Alberti, Bergamín, Gómez de la Serna, Azorín, and contemporary Spanish playwrights: Fernando Arrabal, Angel García Pintado, Agustín Gómez Arcos, Jerónimo López Mozos, José Martin Recuerda, Manuel Martínez Mediero, Luis Matilla, Domingo Miras, Francisco Nieva, Lauro Olmo, Luis Riaza, José Rodríguez Méndez, José Ruibal and Alfonso Vallejo. It is worth noting that many of the playwrights who worked exclusively for independent groups in the 1960s and 1970s are now being regularly produced, with some like José Luis Alonso de Santos, Josep Maria Benet i Jornet, Fermín Cabal and Rudolf Sirera enjoying success with the larger companies. The latter's work *El veneno del teatro* (*Theatrical Venom*) (1983) was a play-within-a-play about theatrical life. José Sanchis Sinisterra, whose *¡Ay, Carmela!* (1988) was later turned into a major film by Carlos Saura, and whose *Lope de Aguirre, traidor* (*Lope de Aguirre, Traitor*) (1992) explored the role of the Spanish state in the conquest of America using texts from seventeenth-century playwrights, is a fine example of this renewed passion for producing work from the sixties and seventies.

In the context of the relatively recent geographical and political division of Spain into autonomous communities, some theatre work has also been used as a tool to explore the historical past and present identity of a region. This has been especially true in Andalusia, Galicia and the Basque Country (Euskadi). A good example of this type of production is Ignacio Amestoy's *Durango, un sueño 1439* (*Durango, a Dream 1439*) (1989). As performed by Geroa, it was a thought-provoking theatre piece of great plasticity which dealt with social events in Durango during the mid fifteenth century.

Spain's growing interest in design is largely due to the visually oriented generation that emerged after the 1960s influenced by the ideas of Roger Blin. Projections are now used regularly in both large and small theatres as a result of their ability to easily suggest space, time and experience; something which has also been accomplished by using light more imaginatively than in the past. Two examples of this are *Comedias bárbaras* (*Savage Plays*) (1992) where director José Carlos Plaza used light imaginatively, and *Ara que els ametllers ya estan batuts* (*Now that the Almond Trees Have Been Picked*) (1990), based on texts by Josep Pla, directed and performed by Josep Maria Flotats with cinematic projections by Alain Poisson.

The increased use of movement in many productions has also led many designers to simply choose bare stages in both large and small stagings/productions. One of the masters in creating a bare stage environment is Andrea d'Odorico, an architect who has a classical and often monumental sense of space. He is primarily interested in the relationship between mass and emptiness and often utilizes chiaroscuro and imitations of marble. His work was at its best in the extremely beautiful design he created for Benavente's *La malquerida* (*The Unloved*) directed by Miguel Narros in 1987.

Despite the attractiveness of the open stage, however, some designers have also managed to create designs utilizing visual suggestiveness, often through lighting. Again, one must acknowledge the work of Puigserver in Brecht's *Mother Courage* (1986), the merry-go-round designed by Frederic Amat for Valle-Inclán's *Tirano Banderas* (1992), both directed by Lluís Pasqual, and a ship created by Montse Amenós and Isidre Prunés for *Mar i cel* (*Sea and Heaven*) (1988), a production by Dagoll-Dagom based on the work of the playwright Àngel Guimerà.

In many other instances, companies have simply chosen to use house ambience rather than a stage. One can even see this now in commercial theatres. This breaking of the proscenium was obvious in such productions as García Lorca's *Comedia sin título* (*Play Without a Title*) (1989) directed by Lluís Pasqual and designed by Puigserver. The tendency to surprise audiences can perhaps also explain the reintroduction of real animals on stage which was a normal practice in the Spanish theatre of the 1920s and 1930s but which has only lately been reinstituted with great success in Salvador Távora's *Alhucema* (1988), a production by La Cuadra.

Designers have also been working with colour more often in the 1980s and 1990s than in previous years. In this area, the work that stands out is again mostly that of d'Odorico and Carlos Cytrynowski, especially in productions of the Compañía Nacional de Teatro Clásico, such as Calderón's *El médico de su honra* (*Physician of his Own Honour*) (1986) in which the designer played with chiaroscuro; *Los locos de Valencia* (*The Mad People from Valencia*) (1986) by Lope de Vega in which the designer used extremely bright tones to suggest the Mediterranean part of the country; and Ruiz de Alarcón's *La verdad sospechosa* (*Suspicious Truth*) (1991) with architectonic fabrics and directed by Pilar Miró.

Francisco Nieva and Pedro Moreno are two designers who have regularly worked with textiles in both set and costume designs. Nieva in particular has used fabrics for special visual and acoustic effects to suggest the sea, sky or blood. Moreno experimented with chromatic ranges in costume and set designs both for the production of classics such as *El alcalde de Zalamea* (*The Mayor of Zalamea*) (1988) and *La dama duende* (*The Phantom Lady*) (1990) by Calderón, directed by José Luis Alonso, and even in more modern plays such as José Bergamín's *La risa en los huesos* (*Laughter in the Bones*) (1989) which was staged by Guillermo Heras at the Sala Olimpia using evocative textual images and a complex semiotic recreation of myth. The production was framed by sound and colour along with accomplished choreography; a striking example of post-modern theatre.

Influenced by oriental aesthetics, some designers have experimented with the expressive possibilities of the human body. Cytrynowski attempted this in his designs for Tirso de Molina's play *El vergonzoso en palacio* (*The Shy Man at Court*) (1989), using bodies as rugs, trees and tables. Gerardo Vera transformed bodies into a fence in García Lorca's *Don Perlimplín* (*Love of Don Perlimplín with Belisa in His Garden*) (1990) directed by José Luis Gómez.

Some groups have made it clear that they prefer non-traditional stage areas such as old factories, funeral homes, markets, subway platforms, garages, train stations and warehouses. The performance group Els Comediants had great success with *Dimonis* (*Devils*) (1983), a collective creation performed outdoors in the Parque del Retiro of Madrid, as did La Fura del Baus company, which performed *Accions* (1983) in the old Galileo Funeral Home in Madrid. In the case of Els Comediants, the use of an expansive outdoor space allowed the director to include fireworks, races and masks, while in the case of La Fura del Baus, the use of funeral homes provoked public outrage because of its connection with the dead.

Six stage directors stand out in Spain during this period: Fabià Puigserver (1938–1991), José Luis Gómez (b.1940), Albert Boadella (b.1943), José Carlos Plaza (b.1945), Lluís Pasqual (b.1951) and Guillermo Heras (b.1952).

Fabià Puigserver,[38] well-known also as designer, emerged from the university theatre movement. In 1976 he founded the Sociedad Cooperativa Teatre Lliure, a pioneering experiment through its combination of the vanguardist theatre with foreign classics. As with Roger Blin, he considered the functions of director and designer as inseparable. He was especially interested in the actor's work with both silence and vocal sounds. He stressed the importance of stage movement with no scenery over classic design and used costumes in order to suggest the historic time-frame. Puigserver directed, with great aplomb, such classics as Molière's *The Misanthrope* (1980); Strindberg's *Miss Julie* (1985); Brecht's *The Good Person of Setzuan* (1988), and Beaumarchais' *The Marriage of Figaro* (1989).

José Luis Gómez García, a director and actor, studied in the Westfalia Dramatic Art Institute and worked with Jerzy Grotowski in Poland. He directed the Centro Dramático Nacional (1978–1980) and the Teatro Español in Madrid. He is an eclectic director who works with different styles of stage direction and utilizes them selectively depending on the

---

[38] G. J. Graells and J. A. Hormigón, eds., *Fabià Puigserver: Hombre de teatro* (Madrid: Asociación de Directores de Escena, 1993).

play. He has chosen classic and expressionist German texts by Büchner, Brecht, Kafka, Handke and Weiss; Spanish classics and historic vanguardists such as Calderón, García Lorca, Valle-Inclán and Manuel Azaña, and interesting contemporary playwrights such as Rodríguez Méndez, Sanchis Sinisterra and Fermín Cabal. He achieved considerable success with Manuel Azaña's *La velada de Benicarló* (*Benicarló's Party*) (1980); Lorca's *Bodas de sangre* (*Blood Wedding*) (1985); Sanchis Sinisterra's *¡Ay, Carmela!* (1987), one of the great commercial successes of the 1980s; *Azaña, una pasión española* (*Azaña, a Spanish Passion*) (1988) and *Retablo de la avaricia, la lujuría y la muerte* by Valle-Inclán (1995).

Albert Boadella Oncins, also an actor, created one of the most prestigious independent Spanish companies of the contemporary era: Els Joglars. His performances were clearly influenced by Marcel Marceau's techniques. He used the actor's work, mime, the use of light, sound and choreographic movement on the stage to express a parodic and satiric viewpoint of Spanish modern society. He worked with plastic artists such as Puigserver, Iago Pericot, Joan J. Guillèn, J. M. Ibáñez, Xavier Bulbena and Josep Maria Turell, as well as musicians such as Josep M. Arrizabalaga, Pau Casares, Josep M. Durán and Rafael Subirach. He earned commercial and critical success in *Cruel Ubris* (1971); *La torna* (1977), which unfortunately brought him a jail sentence; *M-7 Catalònia* (1978); *Laetius* (1980), a striking dramatic realization of a nuclear disaster, considered one of the most significant productions of the 1980s; *Olympic Man Movement* (1981); *Operació Ubú* (1981); *Teledeum* (1983); *Gabinete Libermann* (1984); *Virtuosos de Fontainebleau* (1985); *Bye, bye, Beethoven* (1987); *Visanteta de Favara* (1987); *Columbi Lapsus* (1989) and *Yo tengo un tío en América* (*I Have an Uncle in America*) (1991).

José Carlos Plaza, another actor, was schooled in independent groups directed by Miguel Narros and William Layton: Teatro Estable Independiente and Teatro Estable Castellano. In 1989 he took over the Artistic Directorship of the Centro Dramático Nacional which ended in 1994. Eclectic in his style of stage directing he accorded great importance to the work of the actor with gestures, the tone of voice and group movement, the use of light to create space and time, costume design to present the historic time-frame, and the connotation of symbolic objects. He presented classics by Aeschylus, Shakespeare and Chekhov; the Spanish historic vanguardists García Lorca and Valle-Inclán; the modern Italian playwrights Dario Fo and Ettore Scola; the Spanish absurdist Jardiel Poncela; and the modern Spanish authors Fernando Fernán Gómez and Alfonso Vallejo. *Las bicicletas son para el verano* (*The Bicycles are for Summer*) by Fernando Fernán Gómez (1982), one of the most celebrated productions of the 1980s, was as resounding a success as *Aquí no paga nadie* (*Can't Pay!, Won't Pay*) by Dario Fo (1983), Lorca's *La casa de Bernarda Alba* (*The House of Bernarda Alba*) (1984), Valle-Inclán's *Divinas palabras* (*Divine Words*) (1985), *Carmen Carmen* a musical by Antonio Gala and J. Cadenas (1988), *Hamlet* (1989), and *Comedias bárbaras* (*Barbaric Comedies*) by Valle-Inclán (1991).

Luis Pasqual i Sanchez, also an actor, was educated in the Independent Theatre (La Tartana-Teatre Estudi, Grup d'Estudis Teatrals d'Horta and Teatre Lliure). A disciple of Fabià Puigserver and Giorgio Strehler, he directed most of the Teatre Lliure's productions between 1976 and 1984. In 1984 he took over the artistic directorship of the Centro Dramático Nacional and in 1989 that of the Théâtre de l'Europe. Since 1977 he has directed classic texts by Euripides, Seneca, Shakespeare, Calderón, Goldoni, Musset, Büchner, Chekhov and Marlowe-Brecht. He has also worked with Genet, the modern Spanish writers Espriu, A. Ballester and Gomis; and especially with the plays of the historic Spanish vanguardists García Lorca and Valle-Inclán.

Guillermo Heras Toledo, emerged from the Independent Theatre group Tábano. In 1983 he took over the management of the Centro Nacional de Nuevas Tendencias Escénicas. Well-versed in the principal theories of stage direction, he is very eclectic in his productions. He upholds dramatic writing and concentrates on the direction of actors in gesture, movement in scenery and voices, the plastic connotations of colours in scenery, costume design and musical suggestion. He has also worked as a playwright with narrative, cinematographic, classical texts and essays by John Gay, Brecht, Cervantes, Shakespeare, Brecht, John Gay, Nicolai Erdman, Manuel Vázquez Montalbán and the character of Don Juan. He has created interesting work, diffusing knowledge about several theatrical styles and introducing the work of radical European playwrights including Francisco Nieva, Bernard-Marie Koltès and Steven Berkoff. He pays special attention to modern Spanish playwrights: Alvaro del Amo, Marisa Ares, Carlos Marquerie, Javier Maqua, Rudolf Sirera, and was extremely successful in *Se vive solamente una vez* (*You Only Live Once*), inspired by texts by the novelist Vázquez Montalbán (1980), *Kabarett para tiempos de krisis* (*Cabaret for Times of Crisis*) based on texts by Karl Valentin (1984); Pasolini's *Calderón* (1988); José Bergamín's *La risa en los huesos* (*Laughter in the Bones*) (1989); Koltès' *En la soledad de los campos de algodon* (*In the Solitude of Cotton Fields*) (1990); Berkoff's *Como los griegos* (*Greek*) (1992); and Nieva's *Aquelarre y noche roja de Nosferatu* (*Aquelarre and the Red Night of Nosferatu*) (1993).

Contemporary Theatre Review
1998, Vol. 7, Part 3, pp. 25–56
Reprints available directly from the publisher
Photocopying permitted by license only

Twentieth-Century Spanish Stage Design

John London

This article provides a short history of twentieth-century Spanish stage design. Starting with an introduction to the way in which painted backdrops developed from the nineteenth century, mention is made of important designers such as Amalio Fernández and Salvador Alarma. By the 1920s, the director Gregorio Martínez Sierra had promoted new approaches to design. Dramatists like Lorca, Valle-Inclán and Jardiel Poncela evolved a new aesthetic in written stage directions.

With General Franco's victory in 1939, an ambiguous censorship affected stage design, and even talented designers such as Víctor María Cortezo and Siegfried Burmann came under the influence of the dictatorship. At a subsidized level, technical advances did take place, although the possibilities within commercial theatre remained very reduced. In the 1960s, the Independent Theatre began to encourage an adventurous view of design (taken up by Iago Pericot, for example). Finally, an analysis of the work of Francisco Nieva and Fabià Puigserver shows how other innovative conceptions of design emerged after the end of the Froncoist regime.

KEY WORDS: Stage design, Gregorio Martínez Sierra, Federico García Lorca, Censorship, Francisco Nieva, Fabià Puigserver.

In a long article written in the 1980s, a leading Spanish designer claimed: 'the history of stage design in Spain in a non-history'.[1] Although there had been high points of undoubted interest, the overall picture was one of unrelenting mediocrity. The assessment is perhaps too harsh, but a combination of factors have meant that, in common with many aspects of Spanish culture since the eighteenth century, quality has been based on a reduced number of names rather than a pool of general competence.[2]

---

[1] Francisco Nieva, 'La no historia de la escenografía teatral en España', in *Paisaje intermitente de la escenografía española*, ed. Moisés Pérez Coterillo, Cuadernos *El Público*, 14 (Madrid: Centro de Documentación Teatral, 1986), pp. 4–15 (p. 12). Unless otherwise indicated, all translations into English are my own.

[2] Most of the books and articles referred to in my notes contain illustrations. There are three major archives for set design in Spain: Fundación Juan March, Madrid; Institut del Teatre, Barcelona; Museo Nacional de Teatro, Almagro. On the archive in Almagro, see *I: Inventario: Pinturas, dibujos, escenografías, figurines y estampas*, ed. Andrés Peláez (Madrid: Ministerio

Emerging from the Nineteenth Century

One constant problem is the time-lag suffered by the Iberian peninsula. Whereas the Odéon and the Opéra in Paris had tried out gas lamps by 1822, the Liceo in Barcelona started using gas lighting in 1847 and the technology reached Madrid theatres in 1850. The first electric lighting came to the Spanish capital in 1888, but it was only in 1900 that María Guerrero and her company, influenced by the realism of André Antoine's Théâtre Libre, decided to leave the auditorium in the dark during performances.[3]

Painted backdrops evolved along with the new technology. The Catalan playwright Apel·les Mestres later described the abysmal level of Catalan stage design until the mid-nineteenth century, and his words are equally applicable to the situation elsewhere in Spain:

The wretched 'green room' – for modern plays, the ridiculous 'gothic room' – for medieval ones, the 'Greek temple' which had very little to do with a temple or anything Greek about it – for classical plays, the forest which served as a garden by merely adding a marble fountain to it, or vice versa; and all this invariably focused in the same way – with the viewpoint located in the centre: this was all that stage design amounted to in our parents' lifetime and even when we were young [Mestres was born in 1854].[4]

However, by the end of the century, there were Spanish attempts to codify stage design.[5] If aesthetic levels improved, it was due in particular to the efforts of Francesc Soler i Rovirosa, who worked above all in Barcelona, and Giorgio Busato, who was based for a long time in Madrid.

Soler i Rovirosa's most important practical ideas came from his travel abroad and a continual learning process. In the 1860s he worked for seven years in Paris and was made aware of the importance of lighting for audiences and actors. Following a trip to Germany in 1890, he gave

---

de Cultura I.N.A.E.M./Centro de Documentación Teatral, 1993). Every effort has been made to contact the copyright holders of the illustrations reproduced in this article. The author and editor apologize in advance for any omissions.

[3] See Fernanda Andura Varela, 'Del Madrid teatral del XIX: la llegada de la luz, el teatro por horas, los incendios, los teatros de verano', in *Cuatro siglos de teatro en Madrid*, ed. Fernanda Andura Varela, exhibition catalogue (Madrid: Consorcio Madrid Capital Europea de la Cultura, 1992), pp. 85–115. Margaret Rees gives no documentary evidence in claiming that gaslight was being used in a Madrid theatre in the 1830s. See her 'The Spanish Romantics and Theatre as a Visual Art', in *Staging in the Spanish Theatre: Papers Given at Trinity and All Saints' College, 11–12 November 1983*, ed. Margaret Rees (Leeds: Trinity and All Saints' College, 1984), pp. 27–49 (p. 28).

[4] Apel·les Mestres, 'Salvador Alarma', in Salvador Alarma, *Escenografía* (Barcelona: M. Bayés, [1919]), n.p.

[5] See David Thatcher Gies, *The Theatre in Nineteenth-Century Spain* (Cambridge: Cambridge University Press, 1994), pp. 37–38.

a lecture in Barcelona three years later, defending the need to switch off the lights in the auditorium once a production had started. (The custom was initiated in Barcelona a few years earlier than in Madrid.) His backdrops of rustic interiors and Romantic realistic or exotic exteriors are well removed from the shoddy products of his predecessors.[6]

Giorgio Busato was born in Vicenza and studied in Venice. His paintings of fantastic castles and gardens are noteworthy for their striking colour.[7] Such elements were continued by Amalio Fernández who combined realist colour with a precise control of perspectives not pinned to the centre of the back curtain (Fig. 1). Fernández was the main scene painter at the Teatro Real in Madrid for the first five years of this century. While noted for his highly realistic street scenes, he was also capable of manipulating stage machinery and light for special effects. In a production of Wagner's *Siegfried* in 1901, the noise of the storm and the image of vaporous white clouds won special praise. There was an army of stage hands to move rocks and other contraptions. Five men were needed for the dragon: two pushed it along, another two moved its eyes (lit by red lamps) and another one opened its jaws and made vaporous breath shoot out.[8] Fernández was not the only accomplished designer working outside Catalonia at the time. Luis Muriel y López had a painterly style which was not so realist, but he was nevertheless given to surprising audiences with elements from the real world. A famous production of *Madame Butterfly* contained two live pheasants.[9]

In Catalonia, extravagances of a more advanced kind were devised by Miquel Moragas and Salvador Alarma, both followers of Soler i Rovirosa. They had joined forces in 1888, but for several years before Moragas's death in 1916 most of their designs were in fact the results of Alarma's talent. Alarma's folkloric landscapes and interiors are poetic and imaginative rather than photographic. Some have the eccentric charm of Gaudí's buildings. One of his backdrops for *A Midsummer Night's Dream* gives the trees of the wood their own humanity; the branches and roots

---

[6] See Isidre Bravo's lavishly illustrated *L'escenografia catalana* (Barcelona: Diputació de Barcelona, 1986), pp. 77, 82 and Isidre Bravo, *Francesc Soler i Rovirosa: 1836–1900*, exhibition catalogue (Barcelona: Institut del Teatre, [n.d]). For an early eulogistic treatment of Soler i Rovirosa, see José Francés, *Un maestro de la escenografía: Soler y Rovirosa* (Barcelona: Diputación Provincial de Barcelona/Instituto del Teatro Nacional, 1928). For a general guide to the development of Catalan realist stage design, including English translations, see *Escola catalana d'escenografia realista: 1850–1950*, ed. Andreu Vallvé, 2nd edn (Barcelona: Diputació de Barcelona/Institut del Teatre, 1982).

[7] See *Cuatro siglos de teatro en Madrid*, ed. Fernanda Andura Varela, pp. 312–314, 403–410.

[8] Joaquín Muñoz Morillejo, *Escenografía española* (Madrid: Real Academia de Bellas Artes de San Fernando, 1923), p. 164. For examples of Fernández's backdrops, see *Cuatro siglos de teatro en Madrid*, ed. Fernanda Andura Varela, pp. 320–321, 414–417.

[9] See Joaquín Muñoz Morillejo, *Escenografía española*, pp. 174–176.

Figure 1. A street scene designed by Amalio Fernández. Photo: Josep Parer. © Institut del Teatre, Barcelona.

become anthropomorphic limbs. He was renowned for simulating fires, floods and earthquakes without recourse to real fire or water. Alarma was responsible for the introduction of open-air performances in natural settings. From 1911 onwards he staged a series of spectacular outdoor productions of Catalan plays, incorporating the surrounding trees, rocks, sand or plants into his design. Àngel Guimerà's *Terra baixa* (*Marta of the Lowlands*), for instance, was performed near Sabadell and on the beach in Badalona. Alarma was also eager to contrive technologically new methods of presentation. His 'animated diorama' of 1902 employed lighting, sounds and the movements of shapes. The audience could see the scenes – such as a memorable shipwreck – from the other end of a dark tunnel. Years later in the Tívoli Theatre he created the impression of people swimming in the sea by combining the décor with the projection of film footage.[10]

All this technical wizardry may give the idea of a high degree of sophistication. A manual published in the early 1920s provides an antidote to such optimism. Its author, Francisco Arola, outlines how it is possible to make fog with gauze and flames with long strips of paper (shaken by electric fans and lit up in red), but he goes on to disdain special effects. They are applauded by audiences who are essentially puerile and whose ignorance is impressed by loud noises and ostentatious options.[11] Besides, according to Arola, the general level of scene painting was grossly inadequate:

I have been to theatrical performances in which, in spite of the fact that the play in question included scenes in the court of the king of Corinth, the décor was of a *Doric Order* ... and when I asked the stage designer why he had adopted that architectural order, he answered: 'Because the play is about a Greek subject!'[12]

Arola thus proposes a precise educated approach, backed up by a detailed knowledge of lighting and perspective. Indeed, the stress on varying perspectives in intricate architectural backdrops was a recurring preoccupation (Figs. 2 and 3).[13]

Arola also points out that many realistic effects come to grief because theatre companies are too mean to pay for the required material. Hence steps were painted rather than built. Even furniture, lamps and curtains remained in two-dimensional form to save money. Arola was touching

---

[10] For details of Alarma's work, see Salvador Alarma, *Escenografía*; Joaquín Muñoz Morillejo, *Escenografía española* pp. 229–235; Isidre Bravo, *L'escenografia catalana*, p. 154.

[11] Francisco Arola y Sala, *Escenografía*, Manuales Gallach, 121 (Madrid/Barcelona: CALPE, [1920]), pp. 68–69.

[12] *Ibid.*, pp. 11–12.

[13] See also A. and C. Castelucho, *Escenografía teatral: Aplicación de la perspectiva a la decoración escénica del teatro operando por el aumento visual de la planta de la escena* (Barcelona: A. and C. Castelucho/Miguel Parera, [1896]).

Figure 2. A Roman interior indicating an oblique perspective, by Francisco Arola from his manual on stage design. Photo: Josep Parer. © Institut del Teatre, Barcelona.

Figure 3. Another Roman interior by Francisco Arola from his manual on stage design. Photo: Josep Parer. © Institut del Teatre, Barcelona.

on a common complaint. Luis Muriel y López had protested against the Italian practice of using paper backdrops instead of the usual cloth or canvas ones. There were numerous artistic disadvantages in the procedure, but one major advantage: paper was cheaper. When Amalio Fernández left Spain in 1905 to work in North and South America, he did so because he thought Spanish stage design was being ruined. Companies cut financial corners and quality suffered. In 1910, José María Jordá published a series of newspaper articles about the topic. He concluded that the major problem was not the lack of talented designers of whom there were many, but an overwhelming meanness. Much essential décor was rented instead of constructed for the production in question, and the end results were shabby. 'The art of stage design', he wrote, 'has become a vile industry.'[14]

The Arrival of New Styles

The reaction against such tendencies had already begun in 1898 when Adrià Gual founded the Teatre Íntim in Barcelona. After a visit to Paris in 1901 where he studied productions by Antoine and Lugné-Poe, Gual's designs alternated between forms of Naturalism and Symbolism. It was the Symbolist element which Gual was to develop in subsequent years, as objects from nature became stylized and emotionally resonant (Fig. 4). Gual came under the influence of Edward Gordon Craig and was also a pioneer in early Catalan cinema.[15]

Outside Catalonia María Guerrero and her company had adopted the lessons of Naturalism by using real objects onstage and having solid doors through which to enter and exit.[16] However, it was not until the arrival of Gregorio Martínez Sierra's Teatro de Arte at the Eslava Theatre in 1917 that the figure of the director emerged in Madrid. The stage of the Eslava was only four metres deep and had paper curtains, but the designs at the theatre were among the most innovative to have been seen in Spain. The influence of Max Reinhardt, Meyerhold, Craig and Adolphe Appia was proudly acknowledged in Martínez Sierra's project. He began by employing the stage designers Oleguer Junyent, Fernando Mignoni and José Zamora. Yet the most interesting work came from designers who were at an embryonic stage in their careers.[17]

---

[14] For the comments of Muriel y López, Fernández and Jordá, see Joaquín Muñoz Morillejo, *Escenografía española*, pp. 177, 169, 238–239.
[15] See Isidre Bravo, *L'escenografia catalana*, pp. 184, 191–197.
[16] On María Guerrero, see Ismael Sánchez Estevan, *María Guerrero* (Barcelona: Iberia/ Joaquín Gil, 1946).
[17] The most valuable source of information on the project at the Eslava is the beautifully

Figure 4. A sketch by Adrià Gual for the design of Shakespeare's *Romeo and Juliet* at the Teatre Íntim, Barcelona, 1920.

The painter Rafael Pérez Barradas was born in Uruguay and, having left Montevideo in 1911, had passed through Milan (where he became acquainted with Marinetti and Futurism) before coming to Catalonia in 1913. In his continual search for new styles, Barradas had invented a form of post-Futurist painting he called Vibrationism, in which rounded shapes were repeated or geometrically simplified to communicate the dynamism of movement. His theatre designs could verge towards abstraction, but often have an Impressionist feel.

Manuel Fontanals was another artist whose first contact with stage design came through Martínez Sierra. Fontanals's designs were decorative and imaginative, often making no attempt to portray perspective. Using glittering colours and simplified curved forms, Fontanals established pattern as an essential constituent of mood. In 1919 Fontanals witnessed several productions by Max Reinhardt in Berlin, although a more direct influence from the Austrian director was evident in the work of Siegfried Burmann who was a disciple of Reinhardt and had worked with Reinhardt's designer Ernst Stern. As a consequence of his German background and his cosmopolitanism, Burmann developed an eclectic style ideally suited to Martínez Sierra's art theatre. Burmann initiated a studio at the Eslava where backdrops and designs were made. He ended up painting on a full scale several of Fontanals's designs. Burmann was a master at using lighting to create multiple perspectives. A feature he borrowed from Reinhardt for Spanish productions was the location of actors at varying heights so that dialogue or interaction could take place with characters on different levels. Burmann remained active in Spain until the 1950s and his designs were always conscious reflections on the nature of the play in question and the scenic implications of actors' movements.[18]

Martínez Sierra was not the only one to stimulate alternative avenues of design in Madrid. Cipriano de Rivas Cherif developed different concepts of stage space, influenced by readings of Craig, in several experimental theatre groups of the 1920s.[19] There was also critical support for those attempting to go beyond realist décor. Eugenio d'Ors proclaimed that Naturalism was 'killing the theatre', and Enrique de Mesa wrote of a 'realism so unreal ... that it even paints the shadows of ... the leaves of trees – shadows undaunted by the course of the sun – on the walls and façades of fake rural houses'.[20]

illustrated *Un teatro de arte en España*, ed. Gregorio Martínez Sierra (Madrid: Ediciones La Esfinge, 1926).

[18] For Burmann's work in Spain before the Spanish Civil War, see Ana María Arias de Cossío, *Dos siglos de escenografía en Madrid* (Madrid: Mondadori, 1991), pp. 257–260, 276–280, 283–284.

[19] See *Cipriano de Rivas Cherif: Retrato de una utopía*, eds. Juan Aguilera Sastre and Manuel Aznar Soler, Cuadernos *El Público*, 42 (Madrid: Centro de Documentación Teatral, 1989).

[20] See Dru Dougherty, 'Talía convulsa: la crisis teatral de los años 20', in Robert Lima and Dru Dougherty, *Dos ensayos sobre teatro español de los 20*, ed. César Oliva (Murcia: Universidad

Such protests are a reminder of the general status of painted back-drops for plays in average theatres. Design experimentation within text-based theatre was exceptional. Moreover, in the early 1920s, painted décor remained the norm.[21] Yet this did not have to be conservative. Musical revues were often graced by the participation of designers such as Joan Morales and Lluís Masriera, who used collage and distorted perspectives for a style not dissimilar to some famous American sets by Norman Bel Geddes and Albert Johnson.[22] Here Constructivism, Expressionism and Surrealism were rendered commercial and there was no pretence at realism in two-dimensional backdrops. Musical revues were also the beneficiaries of the latest lighting techniques, while serious theatre was often lit relatively primitively.

There was an awareness in some sections of the press of this sort of disparity. In the newspaper *ABC*, the stage designer José d'Hoy underlined another notion central to improving the contemporary state of affairs:

The modern stage designer has to substitute our antiquated reality by changing stage scenery into scenery of the *spirit of the scenes*, of states of mind, of atmosphere, of subtle essence distilled in harmonious images of light and colour.[23]

Writers of the calibre of Manuel Pedroso, Pérez de Ayala and Manuel Machado added to an informed view of the problems threatening Spanish stage design. Not all the press attention was negative. Enrique Díez-Canedo was keen to mention Salvador Dalí's designs for Federico García Lorca's *Mariana Pineda*, premiered in 1927: they were a vision seen through infantile eyes, yet simultaneously recalling Picasso and intimately linked to the 'spirit' of Lorca's play.[24]

The theatre work of famous Spanish painters is a striking, neglected part of theatre history. Picasso's sets for Diaghilev's productions of *Parade* and *Le Tricorne*, like Dalí's work with Lorca and Adrià Gual, and some of Joan Miró's set designs, are in the mainstream of European experimentalism.[25] Nevertheless, since much of this work by artists was

de Murcia, 1984), pp. 87–155 (pp. 126, 128).

[21] See Dru Dougherty and María Francisca Vilches de Frutos, *La escena madrileña entre 1918 y 1926: Análisis y documentación*, Colección Arte, Serie Teatro, 109 (Madrid: Fundamentos, 1990), p. 51.

[22] Compare Isidre Bravo, *L'escenografia catalana*, pp. 206, 214 and Theodore Komisarjevsky and Lee Simonson, *Settings and Costumes of the Modern Stage* (London/New York: The Studio, 1933), pp. 107, 127.

[23] *ABC*, 24 October 1929; quoted in Dru Dougherty, 'Talia convulsa', p. 127.

[24] Enrique Díez–Canedo, *Artículos de crítica teatral: El teatro español de 1914 a 1936*, 4 vols (Mexico City: Joaquín Mortiz, 1968), IV, 134.

[25] See Montserrat Aguer and Fèlix Fanés, 'Illustrated Biography', in *Salvador Dalí: The Early Years*, ed. Michael Raeburn (London: South Bank Centre, 1994), pp. 17–48 (p. 31): *Miró en escena*, ed. Jordi Fernando (Barcelona: Fundació Joan Miró/Ajuntament de Barcelona, 1994)

carried out abroad, ultimately more important for the development of Spanish theatre was the way in which dramatists started assaulting reductivist, decorative concepts of design. Lorca, for instance, was himself responsible for a few rudimentary sets, although it is in his writing that his innovations found a lasting home.[26] In plays like *Bodas de sangre* (*Blood Wedding*) and *La casa de Bernarda Alba* (*The House of Bernarda Alba*), colour plays an essential part in conveying mood.[27] During Lorca's lifetime, a particularly fruitful collaboration occurred with Siegfried Burmann.[28] In Lorca's more experimental work such as *El público* (*The Public*) and *Comedia sin título* (*Play without Title*), he challenged the whole physical and conceptual structure of existing theatre.[29]

Jacinto Grau would develop stage directions in another area,[30] but the potential for revolutionary sets lay in the work of two playwrights working in very different genres. Enrique Jardiel Poncela was essentially a comic dramatist and his concept of humour extended to his detailed notes on proposed sets. *Eloísa está debajo de un almendro* (*Eliose is under an Almond Tree*), although premiered in 1940, one year after the end of the Civil War, can be seen a culmination of his pre-war plays. Here are some extracts from the stage directions for the first act:

A drawing room – so to speak – in MARIANA's father's house. It is an oddly shaped room as deep as the stage; the left wall runs perpendicular to the footlights, but the right forms a sharp, 90-degree angle halfway upstage and continues parallel to the footlights for about eight feet; at this point, it twists again, slanting slowly but surely upstage. Set into this eight-foot segment parallel to the footlights is an opening six and a half feet wide and ten or eleven feet high, which reveals part of a second room ... As for the furniture, decorations and props, the room could not look more absurd; it looks like a cross between a parlor, a living room and a museum exhibit ... At the foot of the bed are two wide shelves crammed with variously sized cardboard boxes containing a multitude of

---

[includes texts in English translation]. For the strong impression made on a Spanish poet and dramatist by *Le Tricorne*, see Rafael Alberti, *La arboleda perdida* (Buenos Aires: Fabril Editora, 1959), pp. 129–130.

[26] For Lorca's set and costume designs, see Mario Hernández, *Line of Light and Shadow: The Drawings of Federico García Lorca*, trans. Christopher Maurer (Durham: Duke University Press/Duke University Museum of Art, 1991), pp. 87–95, 236–242.

[27] See Gwynne Edwards, 'A Question of Perspective: Staging in Valle-Inclán, Lorca and Buero Vallejo', in *Staging in the Spanish Theatre*, ed. Margaret Rees, pp. 87–120.

[28] See Ana María Arias de Cossío, *Dos siglos de escenografía en Madrid*, plates 96–100; María Francisca Vilches de Frutos and Dru Dougherty, *Los estrenos teatrales de Federico García Lorca (1920–1945)* (Madrid: Tabapress, 1992), pp. 56–59.

[29] Although Lorca's unfinished play is commonly called *Play without Title*, Lorca did in fact intend to call it *El sueño de la vida* (*The Dream of Life*). See Ian Gibson, *Federico García Lorca*, 2 vols (Barcelona: Grijalbo, 1985–87), II, 418–420.

[30] See Dru Dougherty, 'The Semiosis of Stage Décor in Jacinto Grau's *El señor de Pigmalión*', *Hispania*, 67, 1984, pp. 351–357.

bizarre objects: a microscope, a violin, a saxophone, a guitar, a roulette wheel, a typewriter, two or three wind-up toys and a pair of display pistols are the most visible ...[31]

It is as if Naturalism had become manic, concerned with details and objects to such an extent that the three-dimensional aspect of the acting space is absurd, not realistic.

Ramón María del Valle-Inclán's aesthetic vision is more closely linked to his ethical views. The main character in *Luces de bohemia* (*Bohemian Lights*) declares:

Classical heroes reflected in concave mirrors give us the Grotesque or Esperpento. The tragic sense of Spanish life can only be rendered through an aesthetic that is systematically deformed.[32]

Setting can thus be deflated along with characters. Distortion can take place in all parts of the production, costume and set included. In *Cara de plata* (*Silver Face*), first published in 1922, the stage directions appear more related to film than theatre:

The herdsmen ride off, while THE SHEPHERD, high on a crag silhouetted against the sky, waves them off with a shout. In the distance, a flock of doves, flying through the crystal dawn sky, disperse as they soar over the tower of Lantañón.[33]

Behind the mock poetry lies a new mission for the theatre.

The tradition pioneered by Martínez Sierra, of authors involved in theatre projects, continued into the Second Republic (1931–36) when several companies were subsidized by the government. Lorca's company La Barraca, founded to take classical Spanish theatre to areas away from the big cities, was the most famous of these projects. It involved important painters of the period such as Manuel Angeles Ortiz and Benjamín Palencia. José Caballero, the youngest stage designer in La Barraca, later recalled how Lorca created a collective spirit in the company and a new, simple notion of stage design. Both were features absent from the commercial theatre of the time.[34] Sets had to be dismounted easily because the company was itinerant. Santiago Ontañón, another of the designers in La Barraca, went on to make ambitious sets

---

[31] Enrique Jardiel Poncela, *Eloise is under an Almond Tree*, trans. Steven Capsuto, in *Plays of the New Democratic Spain*: (1975–1990), ed. Patricia W. O'Connor (Lanham, Maryland: University Press of America, 1992), p. 29.

[32] Valle-Inclán, *Plays: One*, trans. Maria M. Delgado (London: Methuen Drama, 1993), p. 160.

[33] *Ibid.*, p. 193.

[34] See José Caballero and Federico García Lorca, *Notas sobre 'La Barraca'*, Colección Facsímiles, 4 (Fuente Vaqueros: Casa-Museo Federico García Lorca, 1992), n.p.

for committed left-wing theatre during the Civil War (1936–39). He devised ramps and sloping platforms for war scenes with large casts.[35]

Censorship and Limits in Early Francoism

While General Franco's victory in 1939 entailed long-lasting changes in Spanish theatre, there were also continuities. The left-wing La Barraca, bereft of its first leader, evolved into the Teatro Nacional de la Falange with many of its original members still active.[36] Luis Escobar, the director of the new national company, declared at the outset his opposition to theatrical realism. All the realism that María Guerrero had brought to Spain, with real doors and furniture onstage, was now obsolete 'because it can give us nothing new and because realism denies the very essence of theatre'. According to Escobar, theatre was not real life, and it was stupid to try and pretend it was.[37]

However, this criticism of realism did not at first favour a Surrealist style of presentation. Creative imagination would initially remain firmly within ideologies supported by the dictatorship. The theatrical contribution to the victory celebrations in July 1939 was Escobar's production of Calderón's *La cena del Rey Baltasar* (*Belshazzar's Feast*), surrounded by the statues of the Retiro park in Madrid.[38] These open-air triumphalist productions continued well into the 1950s and played on a nostalgia for the culture of Spain's Golden Age firmly rooted in Catholic orthodoxy. Other Golden-Age plays were performed in front of cathedrals and royal palaces (Fig. 5). (Such productions provided important propaganda material for asserting the popularism of the Francoist regime.[39]) Monumental settings were echoed in indoor stagings which normally involved the image of a central tableau, throne or seat of power on a higher level reached by steps. The pattern was usually strictly symmetrical, thus

---

[35] See Luis Miguel Gómez Díaz, 'Santiago Ontañón, escenógrafo y dramaturgo republicano', *Primer Acto*, no. 232, January–February 1990, pp. 94–101.

[36] See Suzanne Byrd, 'García Lorca's Legacy: Live Theatre at the Battle Front', in *Lorca's Legacy: Essays on Lorca's Life, Poetry, and Theatre*, eds. Manuel Durán and Francesca Colecchia, American University Studies, Series II: Romance Languages and Literature, 138 (New York: Peter Lang, 1991), pp. 205–214 (pp. 212–213).

[37] Luis Escobar, 'Desde aquel tiempo', *Vértice*, no. 25, August–September 1939, n.p.

[38] For a review of the production confirming its role within the newly victorious ideology, see Samuel Ros, 'Un auto de Calderón en los jardines del Retiro y en el año de la victoria', *Vértice*, no. 25, August–September 1939, n.p. Ros wrote: 'Evacuated by the Reds, the soul of Calderón returned to Madrid after centuries...' The same issue of *Vértice* contains reproductions of Víctor María Cortezo's designs for the production.

[39] See Francisco Sanabria Martín, *Política cultural*, España es así, 10 (Madrid: Comisión Interministerial para organizar la participación de España en la Exposición Universal e Internacional, 1958), pp. 44–49.

Figure 5. An open-air performance of Calderón's *El gran teatro del mundo* (*The Great Theatre of the World*), in front of the Palacio Real, Madrid, 1951. Designed by Siegfried Burmann. Photo: Juan Gyenes.

promoting the hierarchy of the Catholic past for the present.[40] There was also a more obvious way of supporting the new regime through stage design. In 1940, Vicente Viudes had the new nationalist coat of arms in his set for Calderón's *El alcalde de Zalamea* (*The Mayor of Zalamea*).[41]

The political transformations enforced a capricious form of censorship which affected set designs as much as writing. The Spanish premiere of Thornton Wilder's *Our Town* in 1944 supplies ample proof of the lengths to which sometimes self-imposed censorship could go. Wilder's picture of life in a New Hampshire village involves actors having to mimic many actions because the set is intentionally minimal. In the third and final act, ten or twelve ordinary chairs represent graves in a cemetery where the dead sit and talk. A procession of mourners later enters carrying umbrellas. The original set is stark, with no perspective imposed beyond the depth of the stage. Víctor María Cortezo's set destroys this quasi-two-dimensional aspect and places the players on varying levels (Fig. 6). The addition of crosses to the chairs brings the play into the boundaries of Catholicism. Yet the changes were not just ideological. By reducing the number of props, Wilder had concentrated audiences' attention on the characters/actors. In the Spanish version, this effect was diluted and the play was rendered more traditional.[42]

When avant-garde staging did occur, audiences often reacted with a hostility reflected by theatre critics who were active in the new system. Salvador Dalí's designs for José Zorrilla's *Don Juan Tenorio* (in 1949) aroused fierce criticism (Fig. 7). Audiences whistled disapproval and one critic thought that stripping the play of its external forms was 'an irreverence'.[43]

Using evidence of official restraints and narrow-minded reception, it is easy to dismiss the 1940s and 1950s as the Dark Ages of Spanish theatre. But to do so is to ignore the accomplishments of several practitioners and the genuine initiatives of renewal. In a trip recalling Soler i Rovirosa's nineteenth-century travels, Cayetano Luca de Tena, head of the Teatro Español in Madrid until 1952, was invited by the

---

[40] For examples, see *Historia de los teatros nacionales: 1939–1962*, ed. Andrés Peláez (Madrid: Centro de Documentación Teatral, 1993), pp. 236, 291, 294, 295.

[41] See Gabriel Ureña Portero, 'La pintura mural y la ilustración como panacea de la nueva sociedad y sus mitos', in *Arte del franquismo*, ed. Antonio Bonet Correa, Cuadernos Arte Cátedra, 13 (Madrid: Cátedra, 1981), pp. 113–158 (p. 124).

[42] For further details on this production, including comparisons with the North-American version and a reproduction of the Spanish set design, see John London, 'Reception and Renewal in Modern Spanish Theatre: 1939–1963', 2 vols (unpublished doctoral thesis, Oxford University, 1992), I, 173–182, II, 443.

[43] Manuel de Cala, *El Noticiero Universal*, 16 October 1950; quoted in Enric Gallén, *El teatre a la ciutat de Barcelona durant el règim franquista: (1939–1954)*, Monografies de Teatre, 19 (Barcelona: Institut del Teatre/Edicions 62, 1985), p. 58.

Figure 6. The final act in the Spanish premiere production of Thornton Wilder's *Our Town*, at the María Guerrero Theatre, Madrid, 1944. Set designed by Víctor María Cortezo. Photo: Ortiz.

Figure 7. A scene from José Zorrilla's *Don Juan Tenorio*, at the María Guerrero Theatre, Madrid, 1949. Set designed by Salvador Dalí. Photo: Juan Gyenes.

theatre section of the Third Reich's Chamber of Culture to study German theatre in 1942. He was deeply impressed by the lighting facilities of the Schiller Theater in Berlin. The revolving stage of the Schiller Theater was the first he had ever seen. In the Deutsches Opernhaus Cayetano admired the facilities for special effects. No technical problems seemed to exist for a theatre director: in five seconds green skies could turn into Gothic cathedrals. After reporting on his visit to the large design workshop of the Opernhaus, and being astounded at the variety of objects constructed, he reflected:

In Spain, a stage is a dirty, dilapidated, dusty place. The simplest operation costs an arm-and-a-leg. Everything is done, regardless of the difficulties, amidst noise and shouting. There [in Germany], to solve a problem, all you had to do was press a button.[44]

Updating these conditions was not without setbacks. When Cayetano used a revolving stage in his 1942 production of Calderón's *La dama duende* (*The Phantom Lady*), the actors were terrified by the new contraption.[45] Other practical advances were less problematic. The lighting technician Rafael Romarate, for example, was fully aware of the varying stylistic functional potential of light angles and intensities.[46]

The set designers who made use of this new technology cannot be simplistically disdained as stubborn apologists for Francoism.[47] Víctor María Cortezo was one of Lorca's good friends. Indeed, he designed the sets and costumes for a production of Lorca's *Mariana Pineda* as one of the events for the Congress of Antifascist Intellectuals in Valencia in 1937. His involvement in the distortion of *Our Town* is as much a symptom of the period as the expression of any personal intention.

Writing in 1943, Cortezo made some observations which acutely define modern forms of expression. According to Cortezo, the modern set designer – in contrast to early nineteenth-century designers – does not try to deceive the viewer. He self-consciously highlights the illusion of the set. Signs proclaiming 'This is a forest', 'This is a palace' can enrich audiences' imagination more than 'the mass of the rhetoric of set design'. Expressionism is an important form, but avant-garde styles only have a function when they fit the tone of the play. Cortezo argues that the realist elements necessary for plays by Jacinto Benavente are 'superfluous for

[44] Cayetano Luca de Tena, 'Ensayo general (notas, experiencias y fracasos de un director de escena)', *Teatro*, no. 5, March 1953, pp. 28–32 (p. 31).

[45] See Felipe Higuera, 'La dirección de escena en Madrid (1900–1975)', in *Cuatro siglos de teatro en Madrid*, ed. Fernanda Andura Varela, pp. 117–143 (p. 129).

[46] See Rafael M. Romarate, 'Luminotecnia escénica', *Revista Nacional de Educación*, no. 35, November 1943, pp. 104–115.

[47] For a good selection of stage design during Francoism, see *Escenografía teatral española*, ed. Equipo Multitud, exhibition catalogue (Madrid: Galería Multitud, 1977), Sections 5, 6, 7.

Ibsen'.[48] It was these tenets that Cortezo would put into practice when the politics of the time permitted.[49]

Manuel Mampaso developed a symbolical approach for his aesthetic. Having started abstract painting in Paris in 1949, he returned to Spain in the 1950s to design some of the most exciting productions of non-Spanish drama and experimental Spanish texts. Premieres of plays by Tennessee Williams, Eugene O'Neill and Alfonso Sastre were designed by Mampaso. It was Mampaso who, with painted backdrops, photographic projections and special lighting, designed the polemical Spanish premiere of Ionesco's *Rhinoceros* in 1961.

Quality design was not restrained to productions of alternative texts. Emilio Burgos's work on *Hamlet* (1949), Victor Hugo's *Ruy Blas* (1952) and Georges Bernanos's *Dialogues des Carmélites* (1954) is characterized by an accurate use of space on a large scale. Burgos's grand architectural structures were at once imposing and rigorous in their focus on actors' movements. It is in Burgos's work that monumentalism is often curbed by artistic sense.[50]

Despite the efforts of Cayetano Luca de Tena and others, the technical possibilities for interesting design remained extremely reduced, especially in the commercial sector where shabby two-dimensional backdrops predominated.[51] When Antonio Buero Vallejo completed *Hoy es fiesta* (*Today's a Holiday*) in 1954, he was unable to find a commercial management prepared to put on the production, since the sets were too complex and expensive and the cast too large.[52] José Redondela, a designer who worked a good deal with unsubsidized companies, would later complain in the press about the lack of time given for preparation and the outdated equipment in Spanish theatres. Sloping stages had been built years before with conventional perspectives in mind. These perspectives were now too limiting if a play or a production required a focus or angle which differed from the traditional view. Although outside Spain, special stage lifts and

---

[48] Víctor María Cortezo, 'Plástica y ornamentación escénicas', *Revista Nacional de Educación*, no. 35, November 1943, pp. 97–103.

[49] For details of Cortezo's career and his working methods, see *50 años de figurinismo teatral en España: Cortezo, Mampaso, Narros, Nieva*, eds. Andrés Peláez and Fernanda Andura (Madrid: Comunidad de Madrid/Consejería de Cultura, 1988), pp. 73–82; *Stage Design throughout the World since 1950*, ed. René Hainaux (London: Harrap, 1964), pp. 12–23.

[50] For examples of Burgos's work, see Juan Gyenes, *Don Juan y el teatro en España* (Madrid: Mundo Hispánico, 1955), pp. 1–8, 45–46, 63–78, 95–100, 111–116.

[51] For an example of such a backdrop, compared to the set of an English production of the same play, see John London, 'Reception and Renewal in Modern Spanish Theatre', II, 433–435.

[52] Derek Gagen, 'Traditional Imagery and Avant-Garde Staging: Rafael Alberti's *El hombre deshabitado*', in *Staging in the Spanish Theatre*, ed. Margaret Rees, pp. 51–86 (p. 52).

other wonders had been introduced, 'here', Redondela lamented, 'we go on working in the majority of cases with hammers and nails'.[53]

Dramatists keen on success and unwilling to follow the audacious precedents of Jardiel Poncela and Valle-Inclán could but conform to prevailing visual norms for the commercial sector, which usually had a comforting bourgeois appearance. In this context it is relevant that the most popular play of the entire Franco period was Joaquín Calvo Sotelo's *La muralla* (*The Wall*): Redondela's set for the premiere production in 1954 established the model for other versions (Fig. 8). Here, Escobar's strictures about realism are overturned. There was just as much ideological mileage to be had by reverting to pre-war forms – free from avant-garde contamination.

Given the stifling political and artistic atmosphere in Spain, it is not surprising that much of the best work by Spanish designers was done abroad. Marià Andreu worked for the Royal Shakespeare Company, the Scala in Milan and Jean-Louis Barrault in Paris. He was the designer of Alec Guinness's controversial *Hamlet* in 1951. Antoni Clavé worked in Paris, London and Chicago, mixing materials and employing the full height and depth of the stage by hanging ladders, curtains or canvas sheets from above.[54]

Escaping from the Establishment: 1960s–70s

By the early 1960s an ambiguous relaxation of original stringency led to large-scale productions of committed dramatists active in the Second Republic. José Caballero's designs for Lorca's *Yerma* (1962) and *Bodas de sangre* (*Blood Wedding*) (1962) show the presence of a form of Abstract Expressionism onstage. But the new decade was also important for the growth of alternative theatre groups.

Fringe activity had been initiated by groups such as El Duende and El Candil (in Madrid) or Teatro de Estudio and Thule (in Barcelona) during the 1940s and 1950s. The 1960s, however, brought a radically different vision which, rather than aping many facets of commercial theatre, rejected it entirely. The groups of the so-called Independent Theatre were anti-Establishment and, in several cases, influenced by the Living Theatre and Bread and Puppet Theatre. Their search for new

---

[53] 'Una encuesta entre los escenógrafos españoles', *Primer Acto,* no. 67, [no month] 1965, pp. 8–11 (p. 10).

[54] For the work of these two designers, see Isidre Bravo, *L'escenografia catalana,* pp. 189, 266–267, 282, 288–289; Anna Riera i Asensio, 'L'obra escenogràfica d'Antoni Clavé' (unpublished memòria de llicenciatura, Faculty of Fine Arts, University of Barcelona, 1985).

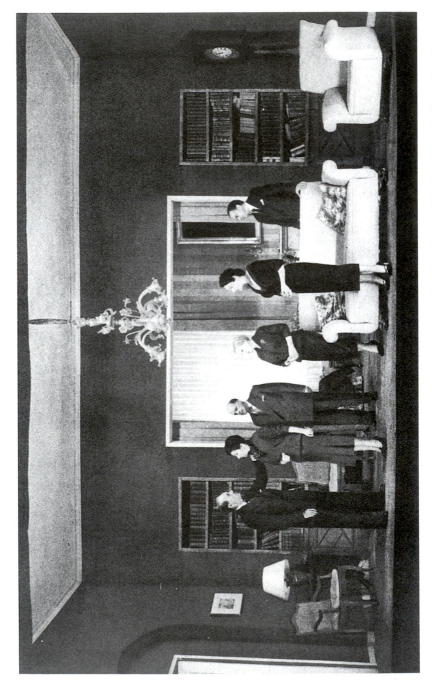

Figure 8. Joaquín Calvo Sotelo's *La muralla* (*The Wall*), at the Lara Theatre, Madrid, 1954. Set designed by José Redondela. Photo: Juan Gyenes.

venues outside normal theatres meant that universities, factories and squares were sometimes automatically part of the set.

The peripatetic nature of the companies and their stress on visual presentation rather than textual fidelity implied a new role for the designer. As Gerardo Vera, one of the young designers of the time, explained, the members of these groups were involved in collective creation and so everybody had to help out with all aspects of the production. The designer could coordinate suggestions to bring about the end result. Vera proposed a design which was functional and anti-decorative, and costumes which could allow maximum movement. Furthermore, the overall style would be integrated into the whole, because the designer was always in contact with the other members of the group. This contrasted with the part played by the commercial designer who brought his sets to the theatre two days before the premiere.[55] Yet there existed a paradox in the alternative professionalism: although more attuned to the particular show, the sets for itinerant productions of the Independent Theatre had – like those of La Barraca before the Civil War – to be easily transportable and adaptable to varying venues.

The work of Iago Pericot is an interesting development from the aesthetics of the Independent Theatre. His set for *Mary d'ous* (*Egg Mary*) (1972) for the Catalan group Els Joglars, consisted of the metallic skeleton of a cube, designed to fit into a small van when folded up. The space became a prison, a love nest and a gymnastic apparatus. Elastic strips sometimes attached characters to the frame. Within Pericot's designs lie a theoretical conception – in some ways related to the ideas of Craig and the Italian Futurists – which redefines the very basis of theatrical scenery. Pericot thinks of the actor as an element of stage design and at one time believed that stage design could have a voice alongside human protagonists. Rather than 'dressing' the play or at best supplying scenery within the mood of the text, modern design could – for Pericot – personalize space. It followed that, in his words, 'any place can become a theatrical space if a dramatic action occurs in it'.[56] The most enterprising enactment of this belief was his setting for *Rebel Delirium* (1977) in the tunnel of a station on Barcelona's metro network. The play, co-written by Pericot and Sergi Mateu, was about homosexuality, and ideally suited

---

[55] Gerardo Vera, 'El escenógrafo y los grupos de Teatro Independiente', *Pipirijaina*, no. 3, May 1974, pp. 1–3.

[56] María José Rague, 'El teatro de Iago Pericot: entrevista', *Primer Acto*, no. 184, April–May 1980, pp. 63–67 (p. 66).

to its surroundings. As Pericot commented, the focus of attention was still 'an *underground* subject' two years after the death of Franco.[57]

Even when Pericot does work in traditional theatres, he uses abstract objects rather than two-dimensional backdrops. For Peter Weiss's adaptation of Kafka's *The Trial*, in 1979, he had a semi-circle of platforms which could change into oblong openings with ramps running from them.[58] While performance groups such as La Fura dels Baus and Comediants are producing the spectacular opening and closing ceremonies to the Olympic Games (1992), it is as well to remember that innovative designers are still changing spaces in conventional theatres.

Francisco Nieva

Experimentalism had begun in a few traditional theatres at the same time as the start of the Independent Theatre, although radically new sets were the result of highly individual talents rather than a general reconsideration of design. The most important figure in this context outside Catalonia is Francisco Nieva. When the veteran theatre critic José Monleón gave an assessment of the subject in 1980, he claimed that, beginning with Nieva, a worthwhile Spanish movement in stage design came into being. A series of direct or indirect disciples expanded what Nieva had initiated.[59]

Nieva spent much of the 1950s and 1960s in Paris and Venice, but returned to Spain in 1964. By 1967 he was expressing the credo which lies at the heart of his approach:

All the force of the most recent European theatre undoubtedly lies in the emancipation from realism ... If Spanish audiences were as 'tremendously realist' as they're supposed to be, instead of a theatrical production, they should be offered a plate of tripe and two spoonfuls of bicarbonate of soda.[60]

Nieva's rejection of realism (in which he included Brechtianism) has little to do with Escobar's panning of realism and the ensuing ideology promoted in early Francoism. For Nieva, a developing theatre is one

---

[57] Patrícia Gabancho, *La creació del món: catorze directors catalans expliquen el seu teatre*, Monografies de Teatre, 24 (Barcelona: Institut del Teatre, 1988), pp. 265–282 (p. 279).
[58] See Isidre Bravo, *L'escenografia catalana*, p. 302.
[59] José Monleón, 'Espacio escénico y escenografía', *Primer Acto*, no. 184, April–May 1980, pp. 13–28 (p. 21).
[60] Francisco Nieva, 'Un nuevo sentido de la puesta en escena', *Primer Acto*, no. 88, September 1967, pp. 48–52 (pp. 50, 52).

which creates a drastic, controversial break with previous forms.[61] And thus, Nieva could never lapse into the triumphalism of Francoist set design for the Spanish classics. In his 1968 design for Calderón's *La vida es sueño* (*Life is a Dream*), he consciously plays with baroque images rather than respectfully glorifying them.[62] Much of Nieva's work can be seen as an attempt to deflate the respected icons of Spanish (and European) culture.

But Nieva is not merely a parodist. He believes that set design has a role which is at once superfluous and essential: 'Real stage design is useless – or it looks as though it is – because it is the only design which is really theatrical.' When everything onstage is authentic, then objects take on too much meaning and, according to Nieva, restrain the imagination rather than stimulating it. Nieva's personal breakthrough occurred when he realized that drama by great authors – such as Lorca, Valle-Inclán and the classical playwrights of the past – could be performed with painted backdrops in old-fashioned or modern styles. On the other hand, realist bourgeois theatre and social theatre needed to limit the senses in order to convey specific ideologies: 'The theatre of ideas, be they bourgeois or Socialist, has transformed theatres into furniture repositories.'[63]

These ideas pervade Nieva's own plays as well as his sets for the drama of other authors. Like Fernando Arrabal and José María Bellido, Nieva demonstrated that opposition to Franco could take a form which was imaginative and ludic. Nieva's 'furious theatre' is, in his words, 'an illegal ceremony', not 'a loud communication with practical reality'. His invented genre of 'reópera' is an 'open theatre for the introduction of forms and reforms of a visual nature: dances, processions, changing, sensationalist set design'. Stage directions exist more to provoke creative reaction than to attain precise images: '*Streets turn into paths and paths break up into the desert* [in Madrid!]'; '*Lightning, without thunder. A few electrocuted birds fall.*' Elsewhere, the silent screen is a strong inspiration.[64]

Nieva's sets tend to be playful through exaggeration. For Peter Weiss's *Marat-Sade* (1968), elements of ruin represented the crumbling

[61] Francisco Nieva, 'El abrupto desarrollo de la escenografía en nuestro teatro', *Boletín Informativo*: *Fundación Juan March*, no. 187, February 1989, pp. 3–12 (p. 12).

[62] See *Escenografía teatral española*, ed. Equipo Multitud, Section 7, n.p.

[63] For Nieva's comments outlined in the above paragraph, see Francisco Nieva, 'La no historia de la escenografía teatral en España', pp. 5, 7, 9, 10, 11. For further information on Nieva's view of stage design, see Francisco Nieva, 'Escenografía de la posguerra en España', in *Escenografía teatral española*, ed. Equipo Multitud, Section 2, n.p.; *Viaje al teatro de Francisco Nieva*, ed. Moisés Pérez Coterillo, Cuadernos *El Público*, 21 (Madrid: Centro de Documentación Teatral, 1987).

[64] For these references to Nieva's plays, see Francisco Nieva, *Teatro furioso* (Madrid: Akal/ Ayuso, 1975), pp. 41, 45, 48, 50, 91.

visual equivalent of the characters' mental decomposition. (Although Adolfo Marsillach's production was performed only four times in Madrid, it remained one of the most exciting shows of the 1960s.) For Nieva's version of Aristophanes's *Peace* (1977), glam-rock antiquated costumes combined with a backdrop of pornography in nature (Fig. 9). In Nieva's *No es verdad* (*It is Not True*) (1988), a reduced décor was nonetheless skilfully atmospheric: wind kept violently blowing open a window and alluding to the savagery outside. Nieva directly attacked the conventions of nineteenth-century realism in his *Te quiero, zorra* (*I Love you, you Foxy Whore*) (1988). The grotesque was at once avant-garde and historical.

Fabià Puigserver

In 1986 Carlos Cytrynowski, the main stage designer for the Compañía Nacional de Teatro Clásico, bemoaned the lack of in-depth training which would be capable of creating a group of qualified professionals.[65] Cytrynowski himself studied in Buenos Aires, and it is no coincidence that Fabià Puigserver, the leading teacher and practitioner of Spanish stage design until his untimely death in 1991, also trained abroad. When Puigserver returned to Barcelona from Poland in 1959, at the age of twenty-one, he had completed a course in stage design at the Warsaw School of Fine Art, and collaborated on productions with Andrzej Sadowski. It is difficult to overemphasize the professionalism of Puigserver's background in comparision to the general situation in post-war Spain. (Although the theatre of Josef Szajna and Tadeusz Kantor is well known, it is also worth noting the extent of those active at other levels: in the 1970s, seven hundred stage designers were working in Poland.)

Moreover, Puigserver is one of the very few Spaniards who always considered stage design to be his vocation, rather than an activity into which he gradually passed alongside other jobs.[66] The need to adapt to untraditional venues during the 1960s forced him to break with certain norms, as he removed the action from the stage.[67] But there are other strands which run through all of Puigserver's work. He is declaredly anti-baroque: 'I want to explain the maximum with the minimum of elements.'[68] His 1963 design for Salvador Espriu's *Antigone* was dominated by a flight of steps which went diagonally up most of

---

[65] 'Seis escenógrafos en torno a una mesa', in *Paisaje intermitente de la escenografía española*, ed. Moisés Pérez Coterillo, pp. 28–46 (p. 46).
[66] See Patrícia Gabancho, *La creació del món*, pp. 305–322 (p. 305).
[67] 'Seis escenógrafos en torno a una mesa', p. 30.
[68] Patrícia Gabancho, *La creació del món*, p. 318.

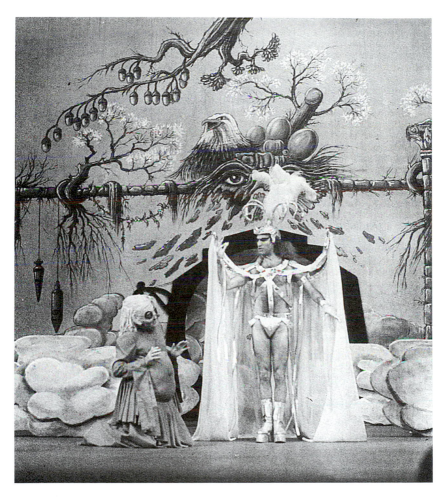

Figure 9. A scene from Francisco Nieva's 'grotesque celebration' based on Aristophanes's *Peace*, at the María Guerrero Theatre, Madrid, 1977. Set designed by Francisco Nieva and the Grupo Escuela Arte Dramático. Costumes by Juan A. Cidrón and Juan Ruiz.

the backwall. For Musset's *Lorenzaccio* (1987), simple, functional steps constituted most of the décor. In Strindberg's *Miss Julie* (1985), plain, unadorned furniture reduced the few objects onstage to an undecorative role.

Puigserver attributed what he termed his 'asceticism' to his time in Poland. However, he also came to admire Catalan designers from earlier generations such as Oleguer Junyent, a disciple of Soler i Rovirosa, and so became integrated into the tradition of Catalan set design. It was part of Puigserver's personal development which took place in the 1960s. He later confessed that he had at first been more concerned to express himself than to establish a link with the dramatic text in question: 'It was a period when I had more professionalism than judgement.' Later, his overt intention was to create a 'cultural atmosphere' which could work in relation to the play.[69] A turning-point in this development was his revolutionary idea for Lorca's drama of a barren woman *Yerma*, directed by Víctor García in 1971. Attached to a frame like a trampoline, a huge piece of canvas provided the main acting area. Actors often seemed engulfed by it as their steps disappeared into the material. It was a membrane and an impenetrable ocean. Parts of it were periodically raised to form hillocks or interior spaces. When elevated higher by one point, the structure became a tent under which characters could congregate. Puigserver himself called it 'an enormous canvas-bladder offering an inexhaustible range of forms, movements and expressions'.[70] The dramatic tension in the text was translated into a visual analogy. Despite considerable success, it was characteristic of Puigserver that he publicly expressed his dissatisfaction with the production. He was worried that the piece of canvas had become a popular gimmick or machine, rather than an essential component of the whole.[71]

Whatever Puigserver's misgivings, his subsequent productions can hardly be considered less ambitious. For *Àlias Serrallonga* (1974) by Els Joglars, the action took place in three separate spaces in the audience: a little theatre, a metal tower (representing a forest), and a platform. In *La setmana tràgica* (*The Tragic Week*), the actors surrounded the audience

---

[69] Quoted in Isidre Bravo, 'Fabià Puigserver, scénographe: élève, agitateur, artiste et maître', trans. Gérard Richet and Myriam Tanant, in the illustrated exhibition catalogue *Fabià Puigserver: Scénographe*, eds. Guillem-Jordi Graells and Giorgio Ursini Uršič (Paris: Union des Théâtres de l'Europe, 1995), pp. 11–82 (pp. 37, 39).

[70] *Ibid.*, pp. 18–19 which also contains photographs of the set and Puigserver's comments on it.

[71] Quoted in Joan Abellán, 'Fabià Puigserver, escenógrafo: 1961–1983 los años decisivos', in *Fabià Puigserver: Hombre de teatro*, eds. Guillem Jordi Graells and Juan Antonio Hormigón, Serie Teoría y Práctica del Teatro, 6 (Madrid: Publicaciones de la ADE, 1993), pp. 195–225 (p. 210). This illustrated book is the most comprehensive collection of writing by and about Puigserver.

all the time, for the acting area went along all sides of the auditorium. Within such spaces, Puigserver varied his style from the Naturalist to the Surrealist and the parodic. Amidst this variety, the self-reference had been eliminated. Art was an act of creation based on life, not art itself.

From 1976 onwards, most of Puigserver's time was given over to work with the Teatre Lliure in Barcelona of which he was a founding member.[72] Following Puigserver's experiments earlier in the decade, the Lliure was the first major theatre in Spain which could be radically modified according to the requirements of each production. (The acting space can be varied in size and position.) Puigserver brought to the Lliure his vast practical knowledge of the materials employed for set design and his meticulous eye for detail. (He always insisted that stage designers should know how to do everything; since the late 1960s he had actually made many of his own designs in Toni Corominas's workshop.)

By the mid-1980s a perceptible return to text-based productions in Spain meant that traditional theatres were once more prized venues, even for experimental performances. But for Puigserver, a theatre always had the potential to be transformed beyond recognition of its original form. When the play in question was concerned with upsetting moral or aesthetic expectations, then the transformation could be all the greater.

Lorca's *El público* (*The Public*) is about the limits of love and theatre. The first stage direction of the play indicates that the room of the opening moments has 'blue scenery'. In 1987 Puigserver was inspired by this laconic indication to remove all the seats from the stalls of the María Guerrero Theatre in Madrid and fill the area with blue sand for the entire performance.[73] Puigserver's interpretation of Lorca combined with Lluís Pasqual's direction. (The two had worked together constantly since the inception of the Teatre Lliure.) Curtains were continually present to highlight the theatrical metaphors of the play. (*El público* also, perhaps above all, means *The Audience*.) Spots and strips of light created acting areas within the larger space (Fig. 10). Shadows became as expressive as actual bodies.

The reflection about the nature of theatre went one step further for the collaboration of Puigserver and Pasqual in the same theatre on *Comedia sin título* (*Play without Title*) (1989). Lorca's unfinished play has little plot. During a rehearsal of *A Midsummer Night's Dream* a revolution starts outside the theatre while discussions on the reality of theatrical

---

[72] For the founding manifesto of the theatre, see *Fabià Puigserver: Hombre de teatro*, eds. Guillem Jordi Graells and Juan Antonio Hormigón, pp. 140–148.

[73] The production originated in the Piccolo Teatro in Milan in 1986 and transferred to the María Guerrero Theatre in Madrid in 1987. For extensive illustrations and details of the production, see the booklet/programme which accompanied it.

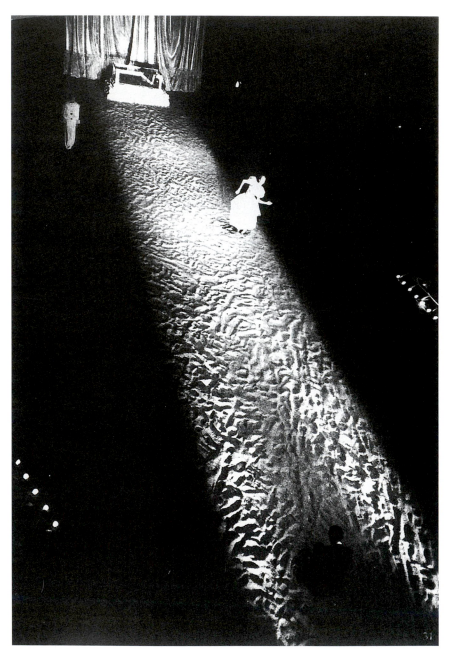

Figure 10. Lorca's *El público* (*The Public*), at the María Guerrero Theatre, Madrid, 1987. Set designed by Fabià Puigserver, with the assistance of Frederic Amat. Photo: Ros Ribas.

Figure 11. Photograph showing a part of the stage of the María Guerrero Theatre collapsing in the closing moments of Lorca's *Comedia sin título* (*Play without Title*), 1989. Set designed by Fabià Puigserver. Photo: Ros Ribas.

interpretation go on inside. Lorca gave little information as to how a production should work, but any impact depends on capturing the immediacy of 'real fear' induced by unplanned events which go on beyond the walls of the theatre. Hence, in a gesture which echoed nineteenth-century practices, the lights of the auditorium stayed on for half of the performance. Lorca's 'Author' directed proceedings from amidst the audience. Actor-members of the audience got up and shouted at those onstage. At the end, a final explosion (from outside) caused the stage to collapse. Sections of the theatre crumbled and a cloud of dust spread over the audience (Fig. 11). People rushed out of the building, scared that something had gone wrong, when in fact Puigserver had engineered the whole event.

More than fifty years after they had been written, Lorca's 'impossible' plays had at last found a team capable of facing their originality. Stage design may have been late in meeting the appropriate demands, but unlike previous delays, this time-lag could be viewed optimistically: the challenges in staging innovations created by a Spanish writer had been met by a Spanish stage designer.

Contemporary Theatre Review
1998, Vol. 7, Part 3, pp. 57–66
Reprints available directly from the publisher
Photocopying permitted by license only

The Function and Mission of Theatre: Ortega's *Idea del teatro*

Stephen G. H. Roberts

This article considers Ortega y Gasset's *Idea del teatro* (1946), the Spanish philosopher's little-known study of the nature and origins of theatre. It sets out to understand why Ortega believes Western theatre to be in a state of crisis and to discover how, in his eyes, its health can be restored. This involves placing the work in the context of Ortega's philosophical outlook, especially his idea that human beings need periodically to escape from the reality of their everyday lives into a world of imagination and 'unreality'. In the light of such ideas, an attempt is made to clarify Ortega's understanding of the true function and mission of theatre.

KEY WORDS: José Ortega y Gasset, Crisis, Mission, Function, Metaphor.

The Spaniard José Ortega y Gasset (1883–1955) is best known nowadays as a philosopher and a political theorist. However, he also played an important role as a commentator on art and literature, believing that he was thereby aiding the cultural regeneration of his country. His numerous works on aesthetic matters are, not surprisingly, profoundly informed by his political and philosophical thought.

This can be seen clearly in *Idea del teatro* (*Idea of Theatre*). Ortega gave this talk first in Lisbon and then in Madrid on 4 May 1946, having recently returned to the Peninsula after more than six years of self-imposed exile from Franco's Spain. His avowed aim here was to renew his dialogue with the young intellectuals of Portugal and Spain and to make them aware of the circumstances of the world in which they lived. He felt that he could achieve such an aim in a talk on the theatre because in his view all forms of cultural expression reveal something about the *zeitgeist*, the spirit of the epoch in which they are created.

He had already attempted something similar in *La deshumanización del arte* (*The Dehumanisation of Art*, 1925), where he had set out to study the phenomenon of what he termed the 'New Art', that is, the work of the

European avant-garde of the early twentieth century. There he claimed that, in contradistinction to the artists and writers of the nineteenth century, who had produced works which invited and even relied on the viewer's and the reader's emotional involvement, those of the first decades of this century were more interested in creating 'pure art', that is, art which called attention to its own aesthetic qualities. The aim of their work was not to mirror or comment on what was lazily assumed to be 'objective reality' but to create new and astonishing realities. This they achieved through the use of metaphor, since, as Ortega noted, 'only metaphor ... can create imaginary reefs amidst the objects of reality'.[1] As a result, the work of the new artists was complex and appealed only to a cultured minority in society. Ortega took this to be a welcome sign that a new elitist note was creeping back into Western culture and society.

Ortega takes a slightly different tack in *Idea del teatro*. Here he does not set out to study the work of individual playwrights or even important trends in contemporary drama. There is no mention of Brecht and Pirandello nor, more surprisingly, any reference to the dramatists of 1920s and 1930s Spain, such as the recently-deceased Valle-Inclán and Lorca. He soon makes clear the reason for this: the theatre, he claims, is in a state of crisis. Like all forms of cultural expression, it goes through periods of good health and decadence. The former periods do not depend solely on the quality of the dramatists but also on the sophistication and insightfulness of actors, set designers and, importantly, audiences. So, he adds, the theatre had enjoyed moments of splendour in Ancient Greece with Sophocles and Aristophanes, in Elizabethan England and Golden Age Spain with Jonson, Shakespeare, Lope de Vega and Calderón, in France with Corneille, Racine and Marivaux, in Germany with Goethe and Schiller, and throughout the whole of Europe during the nineteenth century. Since then, it has been in a state of decline.

Ortega's aim in *Idea del teatro* is therefore to address this crisis in the theatre. And he does this not by discussing the state of contemporary drama but rather by endeavouring to discover the true function of theatre, to define what theatre actually is, its essence, its 'idea'. By doing this, he is taking the first step towards restoring its health and, on the way, as we shall see, he makes some assertions concerning drama which are essentially new and modern in nature.

Ortega's approach to theatre in *Idea del teatro* is very much that of the philosopher rather than the literary critic. And his style reflects this fact: he starts with the obvious, with first principles, and then works dialectically towards profound conclusions.

---

[1] José Ortega y Gasset, *La deshumanización del arte*; found in Ortega, *Obras completas* (Madrid: Ediciones de la Revista de Occidente, 1969), III, 353–386 (p. 373). All the translations in this article are mine.

He starts with the simplest of observations: the theatre is a building to which people go. Its interior is akin to a body made up of two organs: the auditorium and the stage. The auditorium is full of seats and is the space inhabited by the audience while the stage is empty and will be inhabited by actors. The audience's function is to be passive and to see; the actors' to be active and be seen. Ortega can now produce his first definition of the theatre: it is 'a building which has an organic inner form made up of two organs – auditorium and stage – set out in such a way as to fulfil two opposite but connected functions: seeing and being seen'.[2]

Having established these basic facts, he then goes on to reject the classical notion that the theatre should be seen principally as a literary genre, sister to the Epic and the Lyric. Literature, he says, is made up only of words while theatre is more than simply prose or verse; in fact, it is a reality which is not accessible mainly through the sense of hearing: 'In the theatre, we do not only hear; more importantly than hearing and even before we hear, we see' (p. 456). The words of a play are not its principle or defining factor: they are in fact conveyed to us, the audience, through the physical presence of the actors. Theatre is therefore first and foremost vision and spectacle: it does not take place inside us, as happens when we read a novel or a poem, but rather outside us, on stage.

But what is it exactly that we see on stage? Do we see characters and settings, or actors and décor? In reality, we see both at one and the same time, since 'the things and people on stage *present* themselves to us under the guise or with the power of *representing* things and people which are different to themselves' (p. 458). Actors have to be able to negate their own reality and allow characters to inhabit their bodies, with the result that they become transparent and allow other beings to shine through them. In theatre, therefore, that which is unreal – the character – has the magic power of making what is real – the actor – disappear.

Ortega then widens out his argument with the assertion that those realities which have the function of presenting not themselves but other realities are in fact images. As the actors on stage are in essence 'metaphors made flesh', the theatre is primarily concerned with the creation of a world of images, that is, in its most literal sense, an imaginary world. Theatre is therefore, according to this new definition, no more nor less than 'visible metaphor' (p. 459). Once again then we can see just how central the notion of metaphor is to Ortega's understanding of all forms of artistic creation. In *La deshumanización del arte*, he had claimed that avant-garde artists and writers were creating new realities

---

[2] Ortega y Gasset, *Idea del teatro*; found in Ortega, *Obras completas*, VII, 441–501 (p. 455). All further references to this work are contained in parenthesis in the text.

through the cultivation of complex metaphor; here he states that theatre has always been centrally and almost exclusively concerned with the creation of metaphor.

Developing his argument, Ortega goes on to say that the actor on stage ceases to be himself but never wholly becomes the character he is playing either. Both actor and character undermine the reality of the other and, by doing so, create a sense of 'unreality' which lies at the very heart of theatre. Now the creation of 'unreality' on stage is a very delicate operation. A bad actor is unable to convince us that he is Hamlet. On the other hand, naive theatregoers are likely to believe that all that goes on in a play is true or real, a reaction which undermines the imaginary quality of theatre. As a result, human beings need to learn how to watch drama, to read what transpires on stage on a metaphorical level: 'our mind must learn how to adapt so that we manage to *see* that imaginary world of theatre' (p. 462). In short, the audience of a play must be sophisticated enough to appreciate, and join in the creation of, visible metaphors.

Ortega carefully draws attention here to the responsibility of the theatregoer. However, he concludes this section of his talk by claiming that theatre is essentially ludic in character. The audience is – or should be – aware that what the actors do or say on stage is not serious or 'for real' but rather fictional and imaginary. When we go to the theatre, therefore, we knowingly enter a world of unreality and magic, a world which Ortega deliberately refers to as 'farce' (p. 465).[3]

It is at this point that Ortega endeavours to place what he has so far discovered about theatre in the context of his philosophical worldview. The following pages are in fact a reworking of some of his classic philosophical texts, especially *Meditaciones del Quijote* (*Meditations on Don Quixote*, 1914).[4] In this, his earliest philosophical work, Ortega had begun his investigation into the nature of subjectivity and had first expressed the idea that the self cannot be understood in isolation from the world in which it lives and has its being. The dictum 'yo soy yo y mi circunstancia' ('I am I and my circumstance')[5] became the basis of all his later disquisitions on the nature of human life.

Ortega refashions this definition of existence in *Idea del teatro*. He starts with the observation that man has always had a need for unreality, imaginary worlds, game-playing and farce, and goes on to explain that this is so because the rest of human life is deadly serious. 'We are life,

---

[3] We shall be returning to this point later.
[4] The best introduction to Ortega's political and philosophical thought is Andrew Dobson, *An Introduction to the Politics and Philosophy of José Ortega y Gasset* (Cambridge: University Press, 1989).
[5] Ortega, *Meditaciones del Quijote;* found in Ortega, *Obras completas,* I, 309–400 (p. 322).

our life, each one of us his own life', he writes, only to add that 'we have not given ourselves our life but find ourselves submerged in it at the moment that we discover our own being' (pp. 466–67). Furthermore, we are forced to live 'in this present-day world' (p. 467); we may have some freedom of action but we are not able to choose the world in which we have to live. And this world, to use the term coined in *Meditaciones del Quijote*, is 'la circunstancia', our circumstance.

And yet, despite the ineluctable reality of our 'circumstance' and despite the fact that our life has been given to us, 'it has not been given to us made; rather, we have to make it, make it ourselves and for ourselves, each one his own' (p. 467). As human beings, we are therefore faced with a double responsibility: we must make an effort to get to know the world in which we are forced to live and, on the other hand, we must create our own lives by making choices and acting. The simple fact of existing consequently gives rise to a heavy sense of duty and, often, to pain and anguish.

In the face of this sense of duty, men and women need and deserve a periodic rest from life and from living, the chance to escape, if only fleetingly, from the 'perpetual prison of reality or the world' (p. 468). And the only true escape from reality is the one which allows us to enter a realm of 'unreality' which is totally separate from our everyday world. This we achieve through 'diversión' (fun or enjoyment) and, more specifically, through the playing of games, since 'while we are playing we are doing nothing, that is, we are doing nothing seriously' (p. 469). Games are therefore man's route to an 'Ultravida', a life beyond our everyday existence of never-ending and painful responsibility (p. 469).

Now Ortega believes that the Arts (in the widest sense of the word) are the most impressive form of game-playing because they 'free us from this life more effectively than any other thing' (p. 470). When we read a novel, for example, we are taken out of our ordinary lives and transported to a totally imaginary world. But, says Ortega, it is theatre which provides us with the most satisfying form of escapism and which has therefore 'most completely permitted man to escape from his awful destiny' (p. 470). He does not give any reason for his belief that theatre allows us to escape our individual daily reality better than any of the other Arts, but we can perhaps conjecture that it is precisely because, as he said earlier, it is an experience which, unlike the reading of literature or the viewing of paintings, takes place outside us, that is, on stage. However, he goes on to add an important caveat: the theatre has only managed to fulfil this essential function when it has been 'on form' and healthy, that is, at its moments of splendour. He then defines such moments as being those 'when actors, dramatists and the whole apparatus of the theatre have coincided with the sensibility of their age'

(p. 470). The implication, of course, is that contemporary actors and dramatists have failed to do this.

Here Ortega reaches the nub of his argument. To understand it fully, we need to refer back to another of his early philosophical works, *El tema de nuestro tiempo* (*The Theme of Our Time*, 1923). There Ortega had put forward his theory of 'generations', a concept which he believed to be essential to the understanding of human history. Each generation has its own sensibility which it arrives at either by accepting or reacting against those of previous generations. But, of course, in any generation, the vast majority of people simply follow the established ideology while only a minority – the vanguard – set about the task of creating a new one. It is the latter who have the duty of defining their generation's 'historical mission',[6] something that they can only do if they are fully aware of their position in history.

The present generation – says Ortega in 1923 – has clearly failed to do this: 'Only on a few occasions have men had such an unclear view of themselves, and it is perhaps true to say that humanity has never before put up so meekly with forms which are alien to them, vestiges of other generations which do not correspond to their intimate heartbeat.'[7] What present-day intellectuals and artists have not been able fully to appreciate is that, since the end of the nineteenth century, the Western worldview has changed radically. The Cartesian view, which gave primacy to man's reasoning powers and whose object of study was reason rather than the full range of human experience, has been overthrown and replaced with a new desire to discover values in immediate and spontaneous life itself.[8] Human beings' guiding faculty can therefore no longer be reason alone; they need to forge a new faculty which will enable them both to understand life-as-it-is-lived and to analyze and make generalizations about existence. This new faculty Ortega calls 'razón vital' or 'reason from life's point of view'.[9]

Despite these fundamental changes in mankind's worldview, Ortega's generation still clings unquestioningly to the forms of the past: they take a positivistic approach to philosophy and science and accept the nineteenth-century ideal of democratic liberalism at face value.[10] Meanwhile, in the Arts, they still tend to deify culture, to see it as a surrogate religion which turns its back on what is perceived to be 'ordinary' life.[11] The

---

[6] Ortega, *El tema de nuestro tiempo*; in Ortega, *Obras completas*, III, 143–203 (p. 151).

[7] *Ibid.*, p. 151.

[8] *Ibid.*, p. 186.

[9] *Ibid.*, p. 178. This translation of 'razón vital' is Andrew Dobson's. See Dobson, *An Introduction to the Politics and Philosophy of José Ortega y Gasset*, pp. 170–71.

[10] Ortega, *Obras completas*, III, p. 170.

[11] *Ibid.*, p. 185.

result is that present-day institutions and spectacles are no more than atrophied left-overs from former ages, and this has meant that European civilization has lost its spontaneity, sincerity and vitality. Only the practitioners of the New Art, the writers and painters of the avant-garde, seem to have realized that culture should no longer be seen as something above and beyond life but rather as a festive and enjoyable activity. They have learnt that culture should be placed at the service of life and not life at the service of culture.[12] However, these heralds of the new age are few and far between and the majority of artists and intellectuals have not fulfilled their duty which is to discover the present generation's 'historical mission'. Owing to their failure, 'Western man is suffering from a radical disorientation, not knowing in which direction he should live his life.'[13]

These ideas – first formulated in 1923 – help us to understand the conclusion to *Idea del teatro*. At the beginning of the talk, Ortega had intimated that the crisis in contemporary theatre was related to the fact that 'almost everything in the West is in ruins, but not, it must be understood, because of the War. The ruins already existed, were already there. The last Wars [the Spanish Civil War and the Second World War] came about precisely because the West was already ruined' (p. 450). Because of this destruction of Western civilisation – caused, as we have seen, by the intellectuals' failure to discover their 'historical mission' –, all the Arts are in decline. Perhaps surprisingly, Ortega points to the recent work of Picasso in painting and sculpture and that of Stravinsky in music to prove his point (p. 450).

Unfortunately, he does not conclude *Idea del teatro* with any reference to contemporary dramatists. After his praise for the avant-garde artists and writers in both *El tema de nuestro tiempo* and *La deshumanización del arte*, one might have expected Ortega to identify some playwrights who had actually managed to give expression to the new sensibility. Similarly, he could have spoken about those trends in contemporary drama which he most despised, perhaps the continuing vogue of drawing-room dramas and the more recent one of social realism. But he does not. Instead he simply ends by stating that 'neither the set designers nor the actors and authors are on a par with our sensibility, and as a result the magic metamorphosis, the prodigious transfiguration [wrought by theatre] does not normally occur' (p. 471). Contemporary theatre is not true 'farce' and therefore does not provide audiences with a restful escape from their lives or with the taste of an unreal 'life beyond'. In short,

---

[12] *Ibid.*, p. 186. Ortega was to make a similar point in *La deshumanización del arte*; see Ortega, *Obras completas*, III, p. 383.

[13] Ortega, *Obras completas*, III, p. 193.

dramatists and actors have let us down because they have not discovered what the vital function of theatre should be in the modern world and are consequently doing no more than contributing to its 'ruin' (p. 471).

It may seem shocking to us that Ortega should equate theatre with 'farce', but he is of course endowing the term with special meaning. He defines it as 'the realization of unreality' and uses it to draw attention to the fact that, for the duration of any drama, not only the actors but also the audience participate in the creation of an imaginary world: 'The actor is transformed into Hamlet while the spectator metamorphoses into someone who coexists with Hamlet, who witnesses the life of the latter. As a result, the spectator also takes part in the farce; he leaves behind his normal being and enters into an exceptional and imaginary being. In this way, he participates in a world that does not exist, in a World Beyond' (p. 471). By equating theatre with farce, therefore, Ortega is reminding us that it has a fundamental role to play in human life since it affords us a glimpse of an impossible world where, to all intents and purposes, we are let off the existential hook. He obviously felt that this point needed further elucidation and for this reason he later added an appendix entitled 'Máscaras' (Masks) to the main body of *Idea del teatro*. In this appendix, he turns his attention to the origins, or what he calls the 'prehistory', of theatre. Although this section is unfinished, it does allow us to glean more information concerning Ortega's understanding of theatre's true function.

When Ortega talks of the 'prehistory' of theatre, he is referring mainly to Greek theatre whose origins lie in religious worship. More specifically, it was born of the festivals associated with the cult of Dionysus. Such festivals were public affairs which involved not only worship but also poetry, songs, dancing and riotous celebrations. But all these elements – the religious, the orgiastic, the frivolous and the artistic – worked together as one (p. 475). It is true that the drinking of wine was an important part of the celebrations, but the followers of Dionysus also believed that their festival allowed them to come into contact with an all-powerful god who was as unpredictable as life itself.

As a result, the Dionysian festival was the moment when the Greek people left behind their everyday, ordinary world and entered into another world, a 'World Beyond' (p. 476). As Ortega says, echoing the central argument in *Idea del teatro*, 'Man needs periodically to escape from his everyday life where he feels himself to be a slave and a prisoner of obligations, rules concerning behaviour, work and basic necessities' (p. 480). During their festivals, the followers of Dionysus satisfied this need: the wine, the songs, the dances and the awareness of the presence of their god enabled them to 'free themselves from life-as-worry...and to abandon themselves to pure existence and to the belief that something beyond their personalities . . . is enriching their existences and is saving them' (p. 483).

Classical Greek theatre is heir to the cult of Dionysus, both in terms of its forms and its function. The songs, dances and poetry were amalgamated and adapted to create comedy and tragedy while theatre retained the magic and religious aura associated with the Dionysian celebrations. And, in turn, modern theatre has grown out of Classical theatre and, according to Ortega, should still afford the spectator the experience of ecstasy and joy which the Ancients felt on the day of their festival.

In his meditations on Ancient Greece, Ortega has so far simply fleshed out the points he had made in the main body of *Idea del teatro*. At the end of 'Máscaras', however, he adds another essential ingredient to our understanding of the function of theatre. He starts by talking of the role that masks played in the Dionysian festival but soon changes tack in order to remind us that human beings very early on made a radical discovery concerning their lives: they realized that they are 'a reality limited on all sides and in all directions and that they are therefore completely and utterly impotent' (p. 491). This realization led them to imagine another reality where everything is possible and nothing is limited; in short, their awareness of limits created in them an awareness of limitlessness and caused them to long to be what they are not.

Now this duality (impotence – omnipotence) has always been a part of human life, although the form it adopts changes throughout history. As the centuries pass by, human beings are able to do things which previously were not possible. This does not mean that they become better or worse or more or less intelligent but simply that their relationship with reality changes over the years. As a result, it is never possible to say what mankind is and is not capable of; all we can do at any particular historical moment is to discover where the frontier between our real impotence and our imagined omnipotence actually lies (p. 492).

Ortega never managed to develop this argument fully since he left 'Máscaras' unfinished. However, it is quite obvious how it could be applied to his overall understanding of the theatre. It is the essential function of the theatre to provide individuals with a means of escaping from their everyday world, their preoccupations and their sense of impotence in the face of existence. However, as Ortega has said, the frontier between such a world and the world of the impossible and the imaginary shifts from age to age and from generation to generation. According to this view, theatre must constantly modify itself so that it can both point to where that frontier lies and still afford human beings a sense of escape and of joy. If it can do this, it will be fulfilling its true function and it will then be possible to say of theatre what Ortega had previously said about the cult of Dionysus: 'it is the ecstatic vision of a World Beyond which represents the truth of this world of ours. It is the visionary religion' (p. 484).

As was pointed out at the beginning of this article, *Idea del teatro* is very much the work of a philosopher rather than a literary critic. Ortega is not specific in his criticisms of contemporary theatre nor in his view of how present-day dramatists should be writing their plays. From this point of view, it is a pity that he never actually wrote a further appendix to the work which he putatively entitled 'Sobre el futuro del Teatro' (On the Future of Theatre).

And yet what he does actually say opens up exciting and challenging vistas for the theatre. For one thing, he is clearly aware that the theatrical experience involves the meeting of dramatists, actors, set designers and audience and is not solely about written texts. Indeed, he focuses mainly on the question of the audience's participation in the dramatic spectacle and sheds much light on the way in which audiences are drawn into, and are invited to collaborate in, the creation of that spectacle. Further-more, the complex points that he makes concerning the audience's relationship with the play they are watching and the need for them to learn how to negotiate the 'unreality' of theatre throw up interesting parallels with Brecht's understanding of the nature and role of drama.

Finally, Ortega seems to be at his most modern when he reminds us that theatre is first and foremost visual spectacle. This idea, coupled with his emphasis on the active participation of the audience, would seem to announce many of the trends in recent drama. One of these is, of course, the vogue for street theatre which has led groups such as Els Comediants and Els Joglars in Catalonia to return to the Dionysian idea of drama as celebration and festival. It might be interesting to conjecture what Ortega would have made of such groups and whether he would have believed that they were fulfilling their 'historical mission' by rediscovering and reaffirming the joyful and ecstatic function of theatre.

Contemporary Theatre Review
1998, Vol. 7, Part 3, pp. 67–92
Reprints available directly from the publisher
Photocopying permitted by license only

Enrique Rambal: The Forgotten *Auteur* of Spanish Popular Theatre*

Maria M. Delgado

This article seeks to examine the impact of the actor-director Enrique Rambal (1889–1956), a figure who enjoyed great popular success in the period between 1920 and his death in 1956, but who remains conspicuously absent from published theatre histories of the period. Drawing on existing critical material as well as oral testimonies obtained from collaborators and individuals who recall seeing Rambal's work, it will seek to argue why he has been subject to such neglect and indicate his position as a key director of the era.

KEY WORDS: Rambal, Actor-manager, Melodramas, Cinematic theatre, Spanish theatre, Directing.

Recuperation ... is a phenomenon which ... occurs when a dominant or near dominant culture establishes a vision of a national cultural identity which would also include some if not most of the major writers, artists and musicians of the country concerned. It would present their work in such a way as to imply that the essence of their artistic inspiration corresponded with their own conception of the national identity.[1]

Since childhood I have been very influenced by a theatre director called Rambal. This man must have been very important not only in Spain, for I remember Orson Welles in a really old interview stated that one of the great men in world theatre was a Spaniard called Rambal. Rambal designed grand long novels – Jules Verne's *Michael Strogoff* and *20,000 Leagues Under the Sea*, for example – for the theatre and he realized them with fantastic ingenuity. There you would have caverns, mysterious lights, seas with moving waves ... a theatre of special effects.[2]

---

* Dedicated to Maria Irene Fornes and the memory of Carmen Fornes (1891–1996).

[1] C. H. Cobb, 'Recuperación: An Aspect of the Cultural Policy of the Francoist Regime', unpublished, p. 1. All further references to this article are listed in the text. I am grateful to Rob Rix for drawing my attention to this article.

[2] Carlos Saura, quoted in Antonio Castro, 'Entrevista con Carlos Saura', *Dirigido por*, no. 69, December 1979, p. 48.

His was a grandiloquent and marvellous theatre where anything could happen. I've always thought it very Spanish like the classical theatre, I so like; that grandiloquent theatre, of rhetoric and grand gestures, which I'm sorry to see disappear ... a gestural and exaggerated theatre ... That is to say, I think that the only way to realize theatre is through supreme theatricality.[3]

Recuperation

In a brilliant and provocative unpublished paper C. H. Cobb writes of the cultural policy of the Franco regime as 'an attempt to persuade international opinion that they were the civilized inheritors of a cultural tradition rather than the authors of the savage post-war repression of their enemies' (p. 3). It is often erroneously assumed this process took place simply through a rather heavy handed manipulation of the media that involved the promotion of zealous xenophobia, prudish conservatism and strict gender roles, and a celebration of the Catholic values which formed the backbone of this supposedly homogenous nation. Although the crippling effects of the censorship in operation in the aftermath of the Civil War have been well documented,[4] it is misleading and arrogant to construe that somehow Hispanists working abroad were able to rise above such constrictions in determining their own teaching agenda which opposed that which was legitimized by the regime. The subject of legitimization, however, is a slippery one for as Cobb points out, unwitting collaboration with the regime's objectives took place on a whole series of levels with the curriculum's reduction to a series of 'endorsed' texts (pp. 11–12). The regime's lasting achievement lies in the obliteration of the margins, margins which were not really appropriated by those working within Hispanism abroad. Cobb's glance at the list of thesis in Hispanic Studies approved by British Universities up to 1971 finds no examples of any such texts being prepared for edition. Although Cobb does not really concentrate on play texts or theatre productions to illustrate his argument – with the exception of using Lorca's theatre as an endorsed subject area – his argument does provide some indication as to why certain areas of Spanish theatre studies have remained painfully ignored. The regime promoted an image of certain dramatists, perhaps most conspicuously Antonio Buero Vallejo and Lauro Olmo, as radical dissident figures but their plays are often too easily academicized

---

[3] Carlos Saura quoted in Enrique Brasó, *Carlos Saura* (Madrid: Taller de Ediciones Josefina Betancor, 1974), pp. 251 and 256.
[4] For example, Patricia W. O' Connor, 'Post-Franco Theatre: From Limitation to Liberty to License', *Hispanic Journal*, 4, no. 3, 1984, pp. 55–73; and Anthony Pasquariello, 'Government Promotion, Honors and Awards: A Corollary to Franco Censorship in Theatre', *Cuadernos del Aldeeu*, 1, no. 1, 1983, pp. 67–82.

and the theatrical reception of the works abroad has been distinctly muted. Additionally, certainly in Buero Vallejo's case, the works were staged in the major theatres, theatres which were also staging supposed Francoist works. What is perhaps most interesting is that there is a consensus of opinion as to what the plays mean – i.e., they are about individuals struggling against an oppressive regime, that is 'readerly' as opposed to 'writerly' texts where meaning is ever elusive.[5] Ironically, in their emphasis on enouncement, they may therefore have more in common with the officially endorsed play texts of the regime than may at first be apparent. This is not to equivocally deny the achievements of such playwrights, merely to claim that their claims and those of their champions to be forging an alternative discourse of theatre is perhaps not as valid as they may wish.

If radical theatre practice is at least partly determined by the denial of the playwright, or at least the authority invested in the playwright by liberal humanist criticism, practitioners who move away from the written word towards what Artaud termed a 'theatre of deviation from the groundwork of a pre-established text',[6] offer some challenge to dominant traditions. A theatrical heirarchy which places the play-wright as its pinnacle is fundamentally challenged by practitioners who employ the physical and material (as opposed to the literary) resources of the stage. In addition, the ephemeral nature of the theatrical and its gilded artifice renders it harder to fix and read. It is thus not surprising that a figure like Enrique Rambal who chose largely to work within the realms of popular theatre touring the regions rather than simply fraternizing the Madrid stages should have slipped through the 'official' documentation of Spanish theatre in the first five decades of this century.

Enrique Rambal

Despite the fact that a number of prominent performers and directors within contemporary Spain have articulated the influence that the actor-manager-dramatist Enrique Rambal exerted on their own aesthetic, through his magnificent special effects and his fusion of a variety of techniques appropriated from the early cinema, he remains a figure conspicuously absent from all but one of the main histories of the

---

[5] Roland Barthes, *The Pleasure of the Text*, trans. Richard Miller (New York: Hill and Wang, 1975).

[6] Jacques Derrida, *Writing and Difference*, trans. Alan Bass (London: Routledge, 1978), p. 185.

twentieth-century Spanish stage.[7] Perhaps this is partly to do with the fact that histories of Spanish theatre tend, as with historical, political or sociological studies, to be organised around the key date of the Civil War. Rambal's career was effectively established before the Civil War and continued, effectively unperturbed in the post-war years, much like that of his friend, the Nobel Prize-winning playwright, Jacinto Benavente. One could argue, however, that unlike Benavente, he did not achieve the unequivocal critical success necessary to warrant inclusion in studies of the period 1898–1936. In the politically charged climate of the Francoist era his populist apolitical work – largely within the much maligned and generally feminized genre of melodrama – may have been regarded as unworthy of serious study by both scholars of the right and left. Additionally, Rambal left no great body of playtexts or theoretical writings behind him. In a society where such authority is vested in the written word, the absence of such material renders him a figure of negligible importance. Whatever the reasons, there can be little doubt that his spectacular repertory of 1,789 productions[8] made him a legend amongst audiences in his time, and that the last five years have witnessed the beginning of a re-appropriation of a figure whose contribution to twentieth-century Spanish theatre has been fondly acknowledged by a range of fellow professionals, including Carlos Saura, José Luis Borau and Fernando Fernán Gómez.

Enrique Rambal García[9] was born on November 1889 in the village of Utiel in the province of Valencia where his father was in charge of the train station. It is thought that, due to the precarious financial predicament of his parents, he received little formal education being sent out to work in early adolescence to help boost the family's meagre finances. It was whilst working in a printing press that he claimed to

---

[7] For example José García Templado, *El teatro anterior a 1939* (Madrid: Editorial Cincel, 1980); Gonzalo Torrente Ballester, *Teatro español contemporaneo* (Madrid: Editorial Guadarrama, 1957); and Francisco Ruiz Ramón, *Historia del teatro español. Siglo XX* (Madrid: Catedra, 1984). The only real exception is César Oliva, *El teatro desde 1936* (Madrid: Alhambra, 1989) which briefly mentions his successful tours (p. 24), the influence of cinema on his work (p. 27 and p. 101), and his status as one of a number of Spanish artists who chose to work for extensive periods in the Americas (p. 138). There is a brief reference to him in José M. Rodríguez Méndez's *La incultura teatral en España* (Barcelona: Editorial Laia, 1974), p. 89, but this is a flamboyant, grossly generalized study which fails to offer any substantial re-evaluation of modern Spanish theatre.

[8] A figure listed by Fernando Vizcaíno Casas. See Fernando Vizcaíno Casas, *La España de la posguerra (1939–1953)* (Madrid: Planeta, 1981), p. 196. All further references to this book are in the text.

[9] *Quién es quién en el teatro y el cine español e hispanoamericano* (Barcelona: C. I. L. E. H., 1990) pp. 744–745 lists him as Enrique Rambal Sacia but this was actually the name of his son who settled in Mexico in the mid-forties.

have learnt to read, gradually taking on the responsibility of putting together the serialized novels which formed part of the press's bread and butter business. His first visit to the theatre came in 1904 when he was given a complimentary ticket for *Fedora* starring the renowned actress Julia Cibera. The production allegedly made such an impression on him that there followed, so Luis Ureña claims in his romanticized and colourfully anecdotal biography of Rambal, an avid attempt to see as many new and touring productions as possible, even if this meant going without food for twenty-four hours.[10] Joining up with a group of five other *aficionados* he formed a company which rehearsed at his home, improvising with sackcloth and other household items. His early performances in *Juan José* and *El Micalet* at a small venue of one of the city's then numerous theatre societies, attracted the attention of the well known comic actor Manuel Llorente, who then invited him to work with him. He remained with Llorente until 1910 when he formed his own company which debuted at the Teatro Principal de Valencia with *La almoneda del diablo* (*The Devil's Auction*) with Rambal as lead actor, director and producer. He was then just twenty-one years old. He used the proceeds of the season to travel Europe before returning to stage Victorien Sardou's *La corte de los venenos* (*The Poisoned Court*) at Valencia's Teatro Princesa, where he took the role of Louis XIV, and then embarking on a tour of Andalusia and Africa where the reception accorded to his production of José Zorilla's sentimental drama, *Don Juan Tenorio*, was euphoric. Ureña notes an incident at the Teatro Cervantes in Seville where Rambal, taking a curtain call still dressed in the friar's costume of Don Alvaro, was lifted from the stage by an ecstatic crowd of spectators and carried to his hotel on their shoulders (pp. 36–37).

These early years saw a prominent number of productions of classical works, including Calderón's *La vida es sueño* (*Life is a Dream*), and Ventura de la Vega's *El hombre del mundo* (*The Man of the World*), as well as more contemporary pieces – most conspicuously the plays of his friend Benavente. Soon realizing, however, that his production of *Cyrano de Bergerac* could not pull in the sheer numbers that flocked to see his adaptations of sensationalist novels like *Magdalena o la mujer adúltera* (*Magdalena or the Adulterous Women*), he modified his repertoire accordingly, creating the melodramatic productions which were to make him the most famous actor-manager in Spain. Dismissing claims that melodrama was simply not a genre worthy of significant directorial attention, Rambal begged to differ, arguing that its

---

[10] Luis Ureña, *Rambal: Veinticinco años de actor y empresario* (San Sebastian: Imprenta V. Echeverria, 1942), pp. 15–16. All further references to this book are included in the text.

emotional charge rendered it a significant and respectable art form (Ureña, pp. 39–40).

During these years, in association with the impressario and author Álvarez Angulo,[11] Rambal also ventured into crime dramas – allegedly after an anonymous caller brought a series of them to his attention – exploiting a genre which, although popular in Paris in the latter decades of the nineteenth century, had never really enjoyed a similar degree of success in Spain. Although these dramas largely featured characters from popular late century crime fiction, like Sherlock Holmes, Raffles, Rocambole, Arsene Lupin, and Nick Carter, they appropriated the conventions of the melodramatic form in their action filled storylines, formulaic character types and moralistic endings – with good always triumphing over evil. Rambal, attuned to the impact the new cinematic medium was enjoying, however, incorporated into his adaptations a series of magical special effects – thought, in part, to be developed from tricks he had been taught from experienced stage hands – which were to become his hallmark. For a number of years in the 1920s, beginning with *Fantomas* premiered in Melilla, he delighted audiences across Spain, North Africa, and Latin America (and made a veritable fortune) with a series of animated and fiercely paced crime dramas, whose technical effects included walls which swallowed individuals, carnivorous snakes, invisible men, and chairs which moved of their own accord. When the success of this formula began to wane, he turned to a more methodical adaptation of established novels which offered the possibility of extensive stage effects. Shrewdly chosing as his co-adaptors journalists (amongst them Emilio Gómez de Miguel and Antonio Pérez de Olaguer) who were aware of the necessity of providing pacy intriguing episodic dramas rather than strictly faithful adaptations, he offered lavish spectacles which merged high action with musical interludes.[12] Structurally reminiscent of the soap-operas of today in their shifts of mood, their expansive casts, recognizable character types, multiple locations, musical underscoring and appropriate sound effects, the result by all accounts was that of seeing a three-dimensional colour film. He ventured into the realms of cinema at a time when critics were doggedly predicting the imminent death of theatre, reworking the conventions that were

---

[11] Fernando Fernán Gómez argues that it was only after his rupture with Álvarez Angulo that Rambal went in for the *Gran Espectáculo* that became his definitive hallmark. Until then he was largely concerned with small scale melodramas and crime dramas. See Fernando Fernán Gómez, *El tiempo amarillo: Memorias vol. 1–1921–1943* (Madrid: Editorial Debate, 1990), pp. 133–134. I would like to thank John London for drawing my attention to Fernán Gómez's autobiography. All further references to this book are included in the text.
[12] Fernán Gómez recalls the chorus girls who would double as extras playing everything from monks to French revolutionaries, see *ibid.*, pp. 134–135.

Figure 1. The queues at the box office of the Teatro Arriaga in Bilbao in April 1936 indicating the box-office pull of Rambal's productions.

Figure 2. Enrique Rambal, 1954. A signed photograph dedicated to the actor José Luis Lespe. Photograph courtesy of Gabi Álvarez.

generating such appealing moving pictures for the stage. Never travelling with a company of less than sixty and a minimum of twenty tons of luggage, his grandiose spectacles were eagerly awaited, attracting phenomenal audiences. In 1934, the disappointed crowds outside Bilbao's Teatro Campos Elíseos unable to obtain tickets for the sellout final production of the company's run, marched to the place where he was staying to request another performance. As this proved impossible loudspeakers were installed outside the theatre to project the performance to the gathered crowd. As Figure 1 of the queues at the box office of the Teatro Arriaga in Bilbao in April 1936 indicates, Rambal was an idol of the pre-Civil War theatre, enjoying the star status habitually reserved for film idols.[13] The technically competent nature of his productions was not lost on the major film studios and during one of his North American visits, he was invited to Hollywood, an offer he refused to take up, supposedly because he wished to remain in Spain. Although he did work in film in Spain, it was only as an actor in two features: the first a silent film made in 1920, *El crimen del bosque azul* (*The Crime of the Blue Forest*) and the second in 1934, *El desaparecido* (*The Missing Man*).

His three adaptations of Jules Verne's novels, *La vuelta al mundo en ochenta días* (*Journey Round the World in Eighty Days*), *Veinte mil leguas de viaje submarino* (*20,000 Leagues Under the Sea*) and *Miguel Strogoff*, proved amongst his most lasting successes. *Veinte mil leguas de viaje submarino* offered a challenging re-writing of Verne's novel through the employment of a prima ballerina and twelve chorus girls who emerged from the giant shells resting in the sea. Here film merged with theatre as the Nautilus's sinking was accompanied by a cinematic projection of animal life at the bottom of the sea especially prepared by Rambal at the UFA Studios in Naples. Live action juggled with cinematic seascapes to provide a theatrical experience unlike anything else witnessed by Spanish audiences in the late twenties. Such a mergeance of the conventions of operetta with technological innovation and intriguing plot lines (anticipating the blockbuster musicals of today), was also a characteristic of *La vuelta al mundo en ochenta días*, first performed in 1934 with twenty rotating backdrops designed by Asensi and Morales showing different sights around the world. This latter production involved a procession through the central aisle including three constructed elephants and the shifting of the action from the proscenium stage to other parts of the theatre.[14] *Miguel Strogoff*, again adapted by Rambal and Emilio Gómez de Miguel, into a four act

---

[13] Ureña talks of assaults in the queues for tickets p. 128, and of a storming of the stage by an audience in Caracas in 1935 demanding a further performance of their two favourite plays *La dama de las camelías* and *Felípe Derbley*. See Luis Ureña, *Rambal*, p. 128 and p. 133.
[14] For further details see Fernando Fernán Gómez, *El tiempo amarillo: Memorias*, pp. 135–136.

drama of nineteen scenes, featured seventy-five different characters and a multitude of exotic locations in both Russia and Asia.

Witnesses recall an impressive display of theatrical effects in these productions including a forest fire in *Miguel Strogoff* realized, as Ureña explains in the following manner:

The trees are made of iron and holes, with small orifices all along them; inside there are some conveniently arranged flares, which, when lit, project their light outside, giving the impression that the trunks are on fire. Some hemp is arranged in the branches so that when it burns, the picture will be complete (p. 49).

He goes on to explain the realization of another effect: the sirocco in the desert in *Las mil y una noches* (*One Thousand and One Nights*):

This wind stirs up the sands into blinding whirlwinds that knock people and objects to the ground. The reality of this effect is achieved in the following way: at one side of the stage, Rambal puts a set of some twenty circuit-breakers, and next to these, a little gunpowder. At the right moment, the explosions are set off, which light the gunpowder. This produces a lot of smoke, which should then be controlled using some powerful ventilators. People roll around on the ground, the whistling of the hurricane is simulated, and the audience gets the exact impression of a sirocco in the desert (p. 49).

Although he is primarily remembered for his lavish historical adventure yarns, his extensive repertory – he often had up to fifty productions in each season – encompased horror – *El hombre invisible* (*The Invisible Man*), *El vampiro de la noche* (*The Vampire of the Night*), *El fantasma de la opera* (*The Phantom of the Opera*) – classical drama – Shakespeare's *Rey Lear* (*King Lear*), Lope de Vega's *Fuenteovejuna* – historical drama – *Isabel la Católica*, and Alejandro Casona's little known play *El misterio del María Celeste* – and religious epics – *Fray Luis de Sousa*, *El Mártir del Calvario* (*The Martyr of Calvary*). The *mise-en-scène* of this latter production was inspired by recognizable religious paintings and prints, and conceived as an attempt to provide a Spanish equivalent of the famous dramatisation of the events at Golgotha performed every ten years at Oberammergau (Germany) since 1633. First staged in 1921, it received over 5,000 performances in the period up to 1942, making Rambal over six million pesetas – of which the first million were allegedly spent on the set of *El incendio de Roma* (*The Fire of Rome*). Although generally performed as a 12 noon matinee during the Easter Week celebrations where it inspired fevered responses from packed audiences, it is also known that during a ninety day run at the Teatro Municipal in Caracas, *El Mártir del Calvario* played three daily performances on Tuesday, Thursday and Saturday and four on a Sunday (endorsed by the local clergy), helping to make Rambal over a million pesetas.[15] In the late 1940s during a Central and

---

[15] Ureña also lists its twenty-five day sell out run in León and the 127,000 pesetas made in the 1934 Valencia run and a run in 1933–34 at New York's Teatro Rossi. Luis Ureña, *Rambal*, p. 80.

Figure 3. A 1952 production of *Isabel la Católica*. Photograph courtesy of Gabi Álvarez.

Figure 4. The burial of Christ in *El Mártir del Calvario*. Photograph courtesy of Rafael Borque.

Latin American tour, contracted to play in Mexico for a week as part of the Easter Week celebrations, it ran for five months, lauded from the pulpit by the city's archbishop. There are eye witness accounts by members of Rambal's company of audiences breaking down in tears and screaming in fear as Rambal, in an emotive performance as Christ – a role later taken on by his son – was hammered to the cross.[16] There is no doubt that part of the impact was due to its visual opulence. The set had been painted by three artists, Sanchis, Paula and Díaz Peris, and had two-hundred costumes by Miguel Insa (one of Rambal's most regular collaborators). The religious drama consisted of scenes from the life of Jesus Christ. Special effects included Rambal (as Christ) walking across Lake Tiberias, a trick achieved through a sheet of painted canvas stretched and moved to simulate waves by members of the company.

In many ways the early thirties marked the pinnacle of his success. The plays, although sometimes snubbed by the critics, enjoyed popular acclaim. Rambal played to packed audiences and received official recognition – a street named after him in his native Utiel in 1930. (He in turn awarded the proceeds of a local performance at the Teatro Nuevo, renamed the Teatro Rambal in 1933,[17] to the Town Council, who constructed a school which bears his name.) In 1931 the International Congress of Peace and Work held in Geneva awarded him the title of Comendador for his services to the arts and in October 1935 a tribute by fellow artists, including Alfonso Paso, was held at the Teatro de la Zarzuela, the Madrid theatre where he had enjoyed a lengthy run with *La vuelta al mundo en ochenta días*. Tributes continued into the forties and fifties and included the award of a medal for merit in work and a homage in San Sebastian in 1954.

This is not to say, however, that Rambal's career was one of merry fortunes. He suffered some conspicuous and costly failures which almost ruined him financially. A stage adaptation of Blasco Ibañez's *Los cuatro jinetes del Apocalipsis* (*The Four Horsemen of the Apocalypse*) in Paris ended when Blasco Ibañez, then a veritable force on the literary scene, was unable to attend the pre-play lecture. In the early thirties, attempts to mount a musical revue at Madrid's Teatro de la Zarzuela, *París, París*, which involved the contracting of a troupe of English, German, French and Spanish performers, elaborate sets and a costume budget of 387,000 pesetas, also met with commercial failure. Interestingly, it was this production that was formally responsible for introducing the foxtrot to

---

[16] Gabi Álvarez in a private, unpublished interview with the author, July 1994. There were actually two different versions of the script, one by Gómez de Miguel and Grajales and another later version in 1940 by Grajales, Pacheco and Rambal.

[17] The theatre actually burnt down a few years later. For further details see Luis Utiel, *Rambal*, p. 61.

Spain. Although it was later to become fashionable, it failed to impress audiences at the time. Additionally, a serious gambling habit took him to the point of bankruptcy on more than one occasion, and on the eve of a tour of Latin America, Madrid's Gran Teatro, where the company were due to perform their final Spanish performance (prior to departure) burnt down, destroying all the company's scenery, props and costumes. Thus the tour was indefinitely postponed. Although he finally raised the money to relaunch the tour, a disagreement with the company led Rambal to refuse to have anything to do with them, squandering a substantial sum – the profits of his tour of Brazil, Uruguay, Argentina and Chile – on buying up all the places on a boat from Valparaíso to Peru so that he could travel in peace with only a dog for company. A torrential downpour in Cadiz just as he was due to load up his thirty-four ton cargo for a subsequent tour of Latin America destroyed a substantial proportion of the seventy-two person company's sets and costumes, although no one dared tell him about the disaster until the company's imminent arrival in Buenos Aires. A third tour was postponed for two months with dire financial consequences when Rambal suffered serious burns to his legs after knocking over a small stove in his home in Valencia. Additionally, during the Civil War, Rambal was crippled by a shortage of money and materials which restricted his activities to a spell first at Valencia's Teatro Principal in 1937–38 with a limited repertory including *La cabaña del tío Tom* (*Uncle Tom's Cabin*), *Don Juan*, *Los miserables* (*Les Misérables*), and *Las dos huérfanas de Paris* (*The Two Orphan Girls from Paris*), and later at the Teatro Ruzafa in May 1939 where he hired the necessary sets and costumes.[18] In the years immediately following the Civil War he is thought to have spent time in exile in Mexico returning in the early forties with a revised repertory consisting of stage adaptations of popular films. Perhaps the most acclaimed of these was *Arsénico* (*Arsenic*), commonly known by the title of the film it was based on – John M. Stahl's *Leave Her to Heaven* (*Que el cielo la juzgue*). A highly-wrought melodrama, concerning a woman who commits suicide, preparing for her sister to be condemned for her murder, *Arsénico* offered special effects – including the simulated drowning of a child in a lake – and a tense courtroom drama.

Nevertheless, these years witnessed mixed fortunes. These film adaptations ensured he remained a popular box-office draw in Latin America and the regional theatres of Spain. As such he was able to assimilate into his company the eighteen members of the Lope de Rueda company (specializing in children's theatre) which had been based at the Teatro

---

[18] For further details see César Oliva, *El teatro desde 1936*, p. 24 and Luis Ureña, *Rambal*, pp. 200–202.

Figure 5. An attempt to capture the forties American film look. A still from *Arsénico*, Rambal's adaptation of John M. Stahl's 1945 melodrama *Leave Her to Heaven*. Rambal is in the extreme left of the photo. Photograph courtesy of Gabi Álvarez.

Español until it dissolved in the forties. Roberto Carpio, the company's director, became Rambal's directorial assistant, working with him to expand the repertoire, incorporating pieces devised especially for children, including *Cenicienta* (*Cinderella*) and *La bella durmiente* (*Sleeping Beauty*).

It was also during these years that he married for a second time – he had been widowed in the early thirties. His bride was the company's premier dancer Cecilia Cifuentes. Unfortunately, however, the early fifties saw him risk an expensive musical at Madrid's Teatro Lope de Vega where he contracted a costly team, including the costume designer José Zamora (best known for his work with the Follies Bergères in Paris). The spectacular box office failure of this project brought him once more to the point of bankruptcy and he was obliged to let most of the company go. Although he planned to rebuild his fortune with another Latin American tour, he was never able to realize it; dying in Valencia on 23 May 1956, after being run over by a motor bike.

'Rambalismo' – Analysing a Few Remaining Texts and Examining Rambal's Production Aesthetic

The numerous entertaining anecdotes regarding Rambal's tumultuous life which litter Ureña's study render him as breathtaking and irresistible a hero as the protagonists of his swashbuckling productions and threaten to obliterate his undoubted theatrical achievements. The fact that he appears to have been an eccentric character – naming his children, who proved stalwarts of his company in later years, Enrique and Enriqueta; the stream of younger lovers that followed the death of his first wife in 1931; taking himself from extreme wealth to the point of penury on numerous occasions; his reckless antics with and the numerous accidents involving his beloved cars – and that his (cultivated) adventures/persona should prove so entertaining, should not detract from a concentration on his theatrical practices. Although he refused to divulge the secrets of his stage effects, which led to the collapse of his company on his death, it is thought he picked some of them up during his early travels in Europe and Russia. The few play scripts published by Talia in the thirties and forties offer little indication as to how the effects were achieved. They do, however, provide a taste of the style that was to generate the adjective *rambalesco* (Rambalesque).

¡Jonathan! El monstruo invisible (*Jonathan! The Invisible Monster*) first staged in June 1940 and published by Talia in 1944, is a late example of the crime dramas which had made Rambal's reputation in the twenties.

Described as 'An intriguing story of fear and mystery in four acts',[19] it is set largely in interior locations with a smaller cast than his historical adaptations. Written by Eduardo Moreno Monzón and Baerlam, it tells the tale of an invisible monster terrorizing London who has Scotland Yard's finest on his trail. Mystery surrounds his identity as it becomes clear that he is the dangerous Jonathan Maddon, a criminal supposedly sent to his death in 1923 but able, through malevolent means, to ensure that an innocent man take his place. Even the romantic interest of the dedicated policeman, Rex Walton, is brought into the drama as it is revealed that Alicia is the daughter of the executed man. Her mother, disguised as her nanny, finally executes revenge by killing the villain, thus allowing the couple to enjoy a blissful reunion.

As with his later adaptation of Daphne du Maurier's *Rebecca*, this is a romantic portrait of the English as a fundamentally decent law-abiding people – the threat is seen to come from without, i.e., a lone criminal element presented as a sub-human power who joins up with another 'external' force the Jewish moneylender, Isaac Brolsky, an offensively stereotypical portrait which seems to owe a great deal to Dickens's Fagin. The foreign is an undesirable and threatening element which must be eradicated and it is the job of the rational, male policemen – the élite of Scotland Yard – to achieve this perilous task. Sinister atmospherics allowed the audience to experience a 'world' markedly different from the Spain of the time – dangerous, glamorous, and synonymous with that of the popular Hollywood products enjoying success with the Spanish public of the forties.

Venganza oriental (Oriental Vengeance) by Soriano Torres and Rambal, subtitled 'an exotic and dramatic play',[20] and first performed in 1945, provides an analogous vision of the British. Here a vengeful Chinese husband Yuan-Sing, (played by Rambal), takes revenge on his English wife Clara and her lover Eduardo Priestley by poisioning Priestley. Lusting after her sister Carlota, he devises a plot to rid himself of Carlota's fiancée, Ricardo, brother to the deceased Eduardo Priestley. Things, however, do not go according to plan, for Sing takes the poisoned chalice destined for Ricardo, dying as his wife apologizes for her misdemeanour. Descriptions of Yuan-Sing provided by the stage directions (pp. 13, 23–27, 29) clearly seek to place him within the realms of the unknown 'other'. Here an 'Orientalisation' of the Orient (to use Said's term),[21]

---

[19] Eduardo Moreno Monzón y Baerlam, *¡Jonathan! El monstruo invisible – intriga de miedo y de misterio en cuatro actos* (Madrid: Talia, 1944), p. 1.

[20] Manuel Soriano Torres and Enrique Rambal, *Venganza oriental: Comedia exótica dramática*, adapted from the play by Matheson Lang and Marian Osmond (Madrid: Talia, 1945), p. 1.

[21] Edward W. Said, *Orientalism: Western Conceptions of the Orient* (London: Penguin, 1995), pp. 202–203.

presents a ludicrously fictional image of the 'native' as a cruel and vengeful figure who betrays any trust mistakenly placed in him. Nevertheless the image of the British, all safari suits and pristine uniforms, is equally ridiculous and shown through such discursive excess to exist as another construct: the meaning of both dependent on the dialectical relationship existing between them. As with so many of the female protagonists of the Spanish *españoladas* (folkloric musicals of the forties and fifties), the wayward, transgressive woman suffers substantial inner torment which she shares with the audience, repenting before punishment – here the death of her 'true' love and the public disclosure of her infidelity – is executed.

Fabiola o los mártires cristianos (*Fabiola or the Christian Martyrs*), adapted by Tomás Borrás and Valentín de Pedro from the novel by Cardenal Wiseman and premiered at the Teatro Gran Metropolitano in the heavily populated working-class district around Madrid's Cuatro Caminos, gives a highly dramatic rendition of the martyrdom of Saint lnés and Saint Sebastián for a cast of twenty-five. Divided into fourteen scenes (a conspicuously small number compared to later shorter adaptations like *Dracula* and *Rebeca*), *Fabiola* is a moralistic but highly enjoyable account of the perils of decadence and the worship of false gods (as personified by an array of misled and wicked Romans), and the salvation and inner strength offered by adherence to the one 'true' deity – the Christian God for whom all good Christians go willingly to their death. Excessive dogmatism is avoided through a plot that depends on suspense, intrigue and a range of melodramatic devices, (including a dastardly villain, disguise, a lost handkerchief, and a case of mistaken identity) and the scattering of the action across multiple 'exotic' locations including elegant gardens, dark catacombs, a Roman court, and an amphitheatre. Consecutive scenes (always summarized by a brief title pointing to the action that is to ensue) never take place in the same location, thus attempting to ensure the audience remain attentive. The martyrs suffer a range of horrific punishments – sensationally enacted on stage for the 'moral' benefit of the Christian audience – including decapitation (for Saint lnés), and the launching of arrows against the tied Saint Sebastián. The final tableau provides a cathartic experience for an audience subjected, as is the suffering and noble heroine Fabiola, to a torment for which respite comes only through Christianity. Visited by the ghost of Saint Sebastián, who promises vengeance on all those who have thwarted the Christians, Fabiola's conversion provides the emphatic climax of the piece:

The ghost of Sebastián disappears. Fabiola takes a few steps towards him and falls on her knees; her hands clasped together, her eyes looking up towards heaven. At the place where Sebastián's ghost was, a luminous cross begins to appear, each moment more brilliant. And there Fabiola remains, kneeling at the foot of that immense cross, transfigured by the transformation of her human love into divine love.[22]

Gender politics are, interestingly, not as predictable as might be expected. With the exception of Saint Sebastián, men are generally portrayed in a less than favourable light as flippant hedonists excessively concerned with material wealth, political power and the gratification of the flesh. It is the men who are seen as the abhorrent 'other' – excessively pure and righteous in Sebastián's case, and arrogant, manipulative and dangerous in Fulvio's. Women (through the characterization of Fabiola, Inés, and the disguised Syra/María) are representative of order, stability and reason. Interestingly, the only character who articulates 'desire' (apart from the lascivious Fulvio who arduously pursues the adolescent Inés) is Fabiola. Desire however, remains unconsummated, always exceeding the means by which it can be satisfied.

Desire – as well as its allure and its satisfaction – is also a key motif of the 1943 adaptation of Bram Stoker's *Dracula* undertaken by Rambal in association with Manuel Soriano Torres and José Javier Pérez Bultó. Although great emphasis is placed on capturing the supposedly 'authentic' nature of the proceedings – the English are prim, polite and drink tea in a civilized manner at delightful town residences – which would have proved alluringly 'exotic' to a post-war audience suffering economic hardship, names are, as with all his productions set in England, Hispanised – thus Lucy becomes Lucía, Arthur Arturo, Mina Guillermina. The play is shorter and swifter in pace than *Fabiola*. Its twenty-five scenes move from darkest Transylvannia (as represented by various quarters of Dracula's castle) to genteel London (personified by Lucía Westenra's elegant residence) and incorporate a variety of locations including an East European train station and inn, Kingstead cemetery and London docks, Renfield's cell in the sanatorium, and the ruins of Carfax Abbey. The scenes are brief and episodic and rely substantially on the characters explaining the lapses in time and place. The play begins with what is presumably a projection onto a back wall or curtain (although it could also be a backdrop with the material already written onto it) of information on vampires. This device, probably appropriated from Hollywood films, which flashed onto the screen a newspaper headline to contextualize or explain subsequent events, recurs in Scene Thirteen when Dracula's rampage through London is announced by a headline which mentions the disappearance of children who are subsequently found with strange wounds on the throat. It is a technique used also in *Rebeca*, the adaptation of Daphne du Maurier's

---

[22] Tomás Borrás and Valentín de Pedro, *Fabiola o los mártires cristianos* (Madrid: La Farsa, 1930), p. 79.

novel undertaken by the same team in the following year.[23] Here a picturesque postcard of Manderley Castle serves to indicate its awe-inspiring 'splendour' to the audience. It is highly possible that projected film clips (obtained from the Kielg Bross Studios in New York) were used in both *Dracula* and *Rebeca* to provide some of the more elaborate locations. Joaquín Álvarez Barrientos posits that in Scene Five, as Max drives Carolina out in Montecarlo, a short film of a road in motion would be projected, against which Max's still car would appear to be in motion.[24] This technique was also probably used in Scene Three of *Dracula* as Jonatán is driven in a carriage to the haunted castle. It is possible that film was also used again in Scene Eighteen of *Rebeca* to show the diver swimming though the remains of the boat where Rebeca allegedly met her death and encountering her skeleton (p. 43).

   Rebeca, like *Dracula*, is characterized by multiple locations – a high class hotel in Montecarlo, different rooms in Manderley Castle, valley views, rugged coastlines, a courtroom, and perhaps most spectacularly the burning remains of the Castle which constitute the play's final scene:

The interior of the castle. Furniture is burning, the ceilings are caving in, walls are collapsing; and in the living room, tragic and horrible, the demonic figure of Mrs Danvers, still carrying the candlestick. She seems to relish her terrifying agony ... In the midst of the horrific inferno of flames, Mrs Danvers burns; her clothes, her feet, her arms, her face are all on fire but she remains passive, it is as if she enjoys watching herself burn ... And after this Dantesque scene of horror and death, the curtain falls (Rebeca, p. 59).

There are indications from reviews of the production that the effect of flames was achieved, as with the forest set alight by the Tartars in *Miguel Strogoff*, through the cinematic projection of flames against the back wall, fireworks and red bulbs which were inserted into the simulated beams.[25] Backlighting may have been used to provide the illusion of Mrs Danvers being on fire. Although Alfredo Marqueríe, who reviewed the production for *ABC* in 1944, was scathing about some of the tricks, denouncing the outdated painted backdrops and the backstage noise of the stage hands over which the performers had to make themselves heard, he is also generous in his praise for a production which had audiences leaving the theatre claiming they had never seen anything like it in their lives.[26]

---

[23] Enrique Rambal, Manuel Soriano Torres and José Javier Pérez Bulto, *Rebeca*, adapted from the novel by Daphne du Maurier (Madrid: Talia, 1944), p. 11. All further references to this play are included in the text.
[24] Joaquín Álvarez Barrientos, 'Enrique Rambal (1889–1956)' in *Teatro di Magia 2*, ed. Ermanno Caldera (Rome: Bulzoni Editore, 1991), p. 99. All further references to this article are included in the text. See also *ibid.*, p. 11.
[25] Alfredo Marqueríe, *ABC*, 11 June 1944, p. 34.
[26] *Ibid.*

Dracula too depends on a number of sensational tricks. The script is scattered with references to wolves, bats, a brig battling at sea to avoid sinking, and Dracula climbing the walls of his castle like a lizard. There are also two grand crashes – one involving the derailment of a train in the mountains in Scene Twenty-One, the other a ship catching fire in Scene Twenty-Three. Álvarez Barrientos explains how the former was achieved:

The backdrop presented the opening of a tunnel, in black and white; this was lit at the bottom or the centre with a light which gradually became larger through a diaphragm, giving the impression that the train was getting closer. At the same time the sound of an approaching train could be heard. At that moment the sound of the crash, dark, confusion, anguished screams, etc. (pp. 98–99).

These surviving texts provide some indication of the scope of his effects but spectators who saw his productions boast of even more spectacular effects. Fernán Gómez recalls seeing *El signo de Zorro* (*The Mark of Zorro*) in the thirties, dazzled by the intrepid hero's ability to escape a group of soldiers avidly pursuing him by piercing bags of flour with his sword. The white dust filled the stage, confusing the soldiers and allowing the resourceful Zorro to escape (p. 135). Fernán Gómez also writes of a production entitled *Volga Volga*, based on episodes from the life of the Russian revolutionary Stenka Racine, which took place on a pirate ship travelling along the Volga river. His mother, then an actress with Rambal's company, played a maiden kidnapped by pirates who was delivered wrapped in a carpet, and unrolled before an astonished audience (p. 135). Gabi Álvarez recalls the chariot races featured in *Ben Hur* and Rafael Borque a scene from *El Conde de Montecristo* where the hero changes places with the dead abbot and is cast in a sack into the sea.[27] Against a backdrop of projected images of the sea, the Count was seen fighting his way out of the sack and then rising up to the surface – an effect achieved through the use of a double and the technical recourse to a pulley system.

It is thought that these effects were devised and developed in his studios in Valencia. Here he had a permanent staff of designers, carpenters, tailors, and hairdressers with whom he worked intensely for at least two weeks a year over the summer. Some would remain there while the majority of the company went on tour. In an arrangement with RENFE, the Spanish rail organization, he had two reserved wagons – one for actors, the other for set, props, and costumes – which would be

---

[27] Gabi Álvarez, in a private unpublished interview with the author, July 1994. Rafael Borque, in a private unpublished interview with the author, July 1994. All further anecdotes from Gabi Álvarez and Rafael Borque are from these interviews.

attached to the end of trains for domestic travel. It is known that he slept little, often working eighteen-hour days, and that he oversaw all aspects of the theatrical process, supervising the design and construction of all sets and costumes, and organizing and attending all rehearsals.[28] He rehearsed daily (usually for a three-hour period) – the time of rehearsals depending on the hour of the first performance. Although he is known to have performed less in later years, his own reputation as an actor proved one of the company's most lasting attractions. This may have been, certainly in the early part of his career, due to his matinee idol looks and swashbuckling antics (both on- and off-stage). Gabi Álvarez recalls him as a confident, jocular and energetic actor who enjoyed a sharp sense of comic timing and a talent for improvisation that helped remedy the accidents that occasionally occured on stage. He boasted of having been courted by the largest Madrid theatres where he was offered both comic and romantic leads, but reviews tend to suggest that his most conspicuous talents lay in his skills as a master of disguises and his ability to quickly establish a rapport with the audience. The postures struck in the surviving photographs suggest he modelled a number of his romantic and villainous roles on the early silent American films he so enjoyed.[29] Ureña certainly suggests as much when he calls him the Rudolph Valentino of Spanish theatre (p. 143). Álvarez Barrientos believes him to have been a 'grand' and emphatic actor in the nineteenth-century tradition (p. 101). Ureña tentatively admits as much when he makes a brief reference to an affected performance style and a slight tendency to overenunciate (p. 137). Alfredo Marqueríe records a voice defect which necessitated a clear delivery of each syllable.[30] Gabi Álvarez substantiates this argument, as does Luis Maté, who observes that 'garganta' was always pronounced as 'ga-ra-gan-ta'.[31] Judging Rambal's achievements on the basis of his abilities as an actor, however, is misleading. For as Fernán Gómez indicates with his comment 'Rambal was an effective actor for the genre within which he worked but an extraordinary director' (p. 133), his importance lies in his promotion of theatre as a visual rather than a primarily verbal activity. As such, he did not spend great amounts of time working in detail with actors, his primary concern lay with the orchestration of all elements of the *mise-en-scène*. Within the spectacles that Rambal created, the actor was merely

---

[28] Despite the fact that we know from his posters that there was a head of each department. The programme of the 1952 production of *El Mártir del Calvario* lists a head of electrical affairs, a head of stage machinery, a head of costumes, a master prompter, a head of scenery, a head of hairdressing and make-up, and a musical director.

[29] His summer home at Burjasot is known to have had a private cinema.

[30] Alfredo Marqueríe, *El teatro que yo he visto* (Barcelona: Editorial Bruguera, 1969), p. 204.

[31] Luis Maté, quoted in Joaquín Álvarez Barrientos, 'Enrique Rambal (1889–1956)', p. 101.

another graphic component, working in conjunction with a series of other scenic elements to create stage meaning. As such the remaining scripts should serve not as comprehensive documents but as pretexts in the sense that they provided only a point of origin for the production rather than the measure against which the production was to be judged. Actors and scripts were just differing elements in the composition of elaborate spectacles. His use of different systems of representation sought to privilege the visual thereby questioning what Jacques Derrida calls 'a theological stage ... dominated by speech' (p. 235). In the early years of the twentieth century, Antonin Artaud sought, in the words of Derrida, 'to reconstitute the stage ... and overthrow the tyranny of the text' (p. 236). Rambal may not have used the same strategies to achieve 'the triumph of pure mise-en-scène' which proved Artaud's determining factor,[32] but his analogous achievements in liberating the Spanish stage from slavish devotion to the play text is unquestionable.

Rambal's Achievements

Despite the fact that my assessment of Rambal's work with his Compañia de Grandes Espectáculos (Company of Grand Spectacles) has largely concentrated on his scenic practice, there is no doubt that he was also an astute impressario who was able to exploit the fact that the films of the twenties were silent and in black and white, thereby offering 'live' colour cinema/theatre to the motion picture hungry audiences of the time. In the thirties as cinema changed, so did his stage repertory and effects. Taking his cue from film of the day, more and more action took place against the backdrop of cinematic projections. To audiences accustomed to the pace of cinematic pictures and the spatial and geographical cuts which cinema facilitated, Rambal introduced an analogous practice within theatre. His epic productions of the late twenties, thirties and forties characterized by short scenes, large casts, and varied locations were adventurous, daring and capable of inspiring audiences to scream from their seats. César Oliva holds him responsible for inventing theatrical cinemascope before the Americans and for revolutionizing stage effects (p. 101). Fernando Vizcaíno Casas refers to him as the 'authentic forerunner of the grand stage productions' (p. 196), and Álvarez Barrientos as 'a magician of the theatre' (p. 105). An unnamed critic went as far as to claim that, 'had he been born in another country, he would now be a figure celebrated throughout the world',[33] and

---

[32] Antonin Artaud, quoted in Jacques Derrida, *Writing and Difference*, p. 236.
[33] R. A., *Escenario*, 1946, n.p.

A. Rodriguez de León praises him as the only modern Spanish director to achieve popular success for Lope de Vega, Pirandello and Shakespeare.[34] Although no biographical or critical studies of Orson Welles recall his debt to Rambal, he is known to have mentioned to a number of Spanish film critics a fascination for the range of theatrical effects Rambal was capable of generating.[35] Ureña mentions his influence on Ramón Caralt and a Spanish actor named Doroteo Maté whom Álvarez Barrientos mentions is referred to by Mario Vargas Llosa in *La tía Julia y el escribidor* (*Aunt Julia and the Scriptwriter*) (pp. 96–97). Maté too received great acclaim through Latin America for his spectacular productions. Carlos Saura features a direct homage to Rambal's production style during three episodes in *Mamá cumple cien años* (*Mama Turns One Hundred*) (1978). The first, as the eponymous Mamá, is grandly flown down into the expansive living room from the unseen heavens to the sound of popular *sevillanas*; the second a sham 'miracle' sequence, and the third Mamá's extraordinary rise from the dead accompanied by excessive theatrical effects.

Saura is not the only filmmaker to feature references to Rambal in his work. José Luis Borau's 1986 feature *Tata mía* (*My Nanny*) has a remark about his superlative acting skills when the aged Tata, played not insignificantly by the great music hall star Imperio Argentina, refers to the timid Teo's improvised performance as 'divine, better than Rambal'. Although there is evidence that his popularity waned in the forties and fifties when his scenic effects and painted backdrops no longer seemed as magnificent as they had done in earlier decades, actors and technicians who worked with him at this time recalled the professional nature of his designs, the intricate and demanding nature of his stage trickery and the box office 'pull' his name still enjoyed in the provinces.[36]

Although it could not be claimed that Rambal's was an actors' theatre, it is known that a number of renowned actors including Carmen Bernardos, Nati Mistral, Alberto Lorca and José Luis Lespe passed through his company. Gabi Álvarez recalls him as a demanding blocker of action, who expected great physical precision from his performers. Critics may have denounced the shallow characterization which ran through his dramas,[37] but a marked interest in 'character' as psychological construct never seemed a motivating factor in his work. Character

[34] A. Rodriguez de León 'Enrique Rambal, Creador de Grandes Espectáculos', n. pub., 1956, n.p.
[35] Emilio Sanz de Soto mentioned to me in June 1990 once hearing Orson Welles say as much to a group of critics in the 1960s. Carlos Saura told me that he remembered reading a published interview with Welles where he recalls Welles mentioned Rambal. I have not, to date, been able to trace this interview.
[36] See César Oliva, *El teatro desde el 36*, pp. 27–28.
[37] See Joaquín Álvarez Barrientos, 'Enrique Rambal (1889–1956)', p. 99.

was effectively of secondary importance. Through his orchestration of the characters and action like a puppet-master (or 'master storyteller' as Saura refers to him[38]) Rambal aspired to a different type of theatre where the visual is a discourse in itself as opposed to a means of illustrating the verbal. He drew on characteristics which the Spanish theatre in its striving for naturalist perfection had lost. Rambal showed the possibilities that theatre still offered as spectacle, as a means of bringing together an entire community to participate in the type of theatrical pageants visible before theatre moved into indoor spaces – for entrepreneurial reasons at the end of the sixteenth century – when as Elaine Aston and George Savona note, 'the distinction between the real and the role was progressively blurred'.[39] Rambal's spectacles did not attempt to hide their status as dramatic artefacts. On the contrary, they glorified in their own recognition of their existence as 'writing', in many cases depending or at least exploiting as a marketing tool the audience's prior knowledge of a referent – as with the theatrical adaptations of American cinematic successes. There was no attempt to exclude the spectator on the part of the actor, no attempt to pretend, as in the work of classic realist writers, that the audience is an invisible witness. Rambal's theatre actively encouraged audience participation. Gabi Álvarez, Rambal's *primera dama* during the fifties, has spoken of audience members screaming out directions and advice in the hope of reuniting the two orphan girls in his 1955 production of *Las dos huérfanas de París*. The directions displayed an awareness on the audience's part of the space as theatre, as opposed to 'life'. The audience were agitated and aroused, stimulated and provoked rather than soothed. The local extras – often up to a hundred – employed during the tours ensured 'participation' on a series of levels in a systematic manner unseen for centuries. In the difficult years of the post-Civil War period the pleasure offered to a significant proportion of the population by Rambal's productions should not be underestimated. Rambal provided a celebration of the *jouissance* of theatre.[40] The baroque *mise-en-scène* and open episodic non-linear nature of Rambal's productions offered a theatrical aesthetic which saw theatre as a communal rather than an elitist activity, and where pleasure was the dominant imperative. At a time of falling audiences he maintained a widespread interest in the attractions of live performance, even if his methods involved a recourse to the iconography

---

[38] Carlos Saura, in a private unpublished interview with the author, June 1990.

[39] Elaine Aston and George Savona, *Theatre as Sign System: A Semiotics of Text and Performance* (London: Routledge, 1991), p. 46.

[40] Roland Barthes termed *jouissance* the bliss to be gained from the open-ended, fragmented 'writerly' text, in opposition to the *plaisir* offered by the more cohesive 'readerly' text. For further details see Roland Barthes, *The Pleasure of the Text*.

and techniques of the cinema. In a recent interview the contemporary American director Peter Sellars spoke of theatre borrowing from film at the end of this century 'to keep going' just as film had borrowed from theatre a century earlier 'to get itself started'.[41] Rambal anticipated current mixed media theatre practice with his appropriation and utilization of film. He took risks when other companies preached frugality and economy – risks which Álvarez Barrientos states sometimes necessitated a splitting of the company in two to fulfil all contractual obligations (p. 104).[42] The absence of legislation regarding the number of permitted daily performances allowed Rambal to provide three or even four performances a day. As such he was able to accommodate huge audience numbers. Additionally, he appealed not simply to the middle-classes which populated the fashionable theatres of Madrid and Barcelona but also to the workers and peasants who travelled from distant towns and villages to catch sight of his productions. He himself argued that he succeeded in winning over an audience through his popular adaptations of successful films and novels of the time. The audience were then willing to watch the company perform classic pieces like Rostand's *Cyrano de Bergerac*, Calderón's *El príncipe constante* (*The Constant Prince*), and Benavente's adaptation of Shakespeare's *King Lear*.[43] It is hard to think of another Spanish theatre practitioner, excluding Lorca, who aspired to such a radical agenda or enjoyed such a profound impact across the class divide.[44]

---

[41] 'Peter Sellars in Conversation with Michael Billington at the Royal Exchange Theatre, Manchester', in *In Contact with the gods?: Directors talk theatre*, eds. Maria M. Delgado and Paul Heritage (Manchester: Manchester University Press, 1996), p. 228.

[42] Rafael Borque mentions that Rambal had two different designs for *Don Juan Tenorio*: one for larger theatres and another for smaller venues. As such when asked by a theatre in Murcia to return with *Don Juan Tenorio*, he remained with the production in Alicante, sending half the company with a new production which he blocked in two days.

[43] Alfredo Marqueríe in *El teatro que yo he visto*, p. 205, writes of him 'moving the masses' with his classical productions.

[44] I am grateful to Gabi Álvarez, Rafael Borque, Julia Butrón, Carlos Saura, and Emilio Sanz de Soto for sharing with me their experiences of working with Rambal or viewing his work. I wish to acknowledge the assistance received from the Manchester Metropolitan University who funded a trip to Spain in July 1994 to undertake research for this article. I am also grateful to the staff at the Biblioteca Juan March, Madrid, and the Institut del Teatre, Barcelona, and to Mercè Saumell and José Ocaña for their hospitality during my time in both cities. David George and Paul Heritage offered comments on an earlier draft of this article and I am grateful to them both for their informative suggestions.

Contemporary Theatre Review
1998, Vol. 7, Part 3, pp. 93–107
Reprints available directly from the publisher
Photocopying permitted by license only

Spanish Sources of Fernando Arrabal's Theatre of the Grotesque: Goya, Valle-Inclán and Buñuel

Peter L. Podol

This article seeks to demonstrate the central role that the grotesque plays in the theatre of Fernando Arrabal and to consider some of the Spanish artists whose work shaped his use of that aesthetic mode. Francisco de Goya emerges as the pivotal figure whose paintings and etchings provided the impetus for a number of twentieth-century luminaries working in several different media. Goya's work along with the *esperpentos* of Ramón del Valle-Inclán and the films of Luis Buñuel influenced Arrabal, whose unique form of total theatre in the spirit of Antonin Artaud combined the ideas of that French theorist with the dark humour, scatology and blasphemy of his Spanish predecessors.

KEY WORDS: Fernando Arrabal, Grotesque, Valle-Inclán, Blasphemy, Goya, Buñuel.

Spanish art and literature have made extensive use of the grotesque throughout the centuries. Wolfgang Kayser, in his classic study, *The Grotesque in Art and Literature*,[1] affirms this observation in devoting considerable attention to Spanish artists and writers, from Velázquez and Goya to Gómez de la Serna and García Lorca. This affinity for the grotesque is not surprising in a land choked by traditionalism and repression and noted for its Inquisition, its Civil War and for periods of absolutist terror and dictatorial regimes. As Philip Thomson states in his assessment of the function of the grotesque: 'Because of its impact, it can jolt the reader out of accustomed ways of perceiving the world and confront him with a radically different, disturbing perspective.'[2]

---

[1] Wolfang Kayser, *The Grotesque in Art and Literature* (Bloomington: Indiana University Press, 1963).
[2] Philip Thomson, *The Grotesque* (London: Methuen and Co., 1972), p. 58.

93

Paul Ilie further emphasizes the pivotal role of social reality in providing the impetus for the use of the grotesque in Spain when he observes: 'Social reality has always been transformed by the artist, but only in modern times has it been systematically disfigured. This is why we must place so much importance on the Spanish grotesque within the European context of discords. For Spain has produced a grotesque not only by literary convention but by cultural reality.'[3] A number of works of Spanish art and literature, from the Middle Ages through the present, attest to Spain's penchant for the grotesque: Juan Ruiz's *Libro de buen amor*, Fernando de Rojas' *La Celestina*, the picaresque novel, Velázquez's paintings of the dwarfs in the court of Phillip IV, and the prose fiction of Francisco Quevedo and Miguel de Cervantes. But the figure who laid the groundwork for the modern grotesque in Spain is undoubtedly Francisco de Goya. This study will examine briefly Goya's use of the grotesque in the *Caprichos* and the subsequent impact of his work on Ramón del Valle-Inclán, Luis Buñuel and especially on Fernando Arrabal, the playwright and filmmaker whose work integrates and expands upon that of previous artists in its utilization of that aesthetic mode. Because of Arrabal's lengthy period of self-exile in France,[4] critics have sometimes categorized him as a French playwright. However, his use of black humour and the grotesque in conjunction with his choice of themes and the incorporation of rituals and ceremonies inspired by the Catholic Church into his theatre clearly identify him with Spain and justify his central role in this consideration of the modern Spanish grotesque.

In his study of the grotesque, Geoffrey Harpham emphasizes the central role played by dissonance in style and subject matter. As he states: 'The grotesque often arises in the clash between the 'virtuoso' limitations of form and a rebellious content that refuses to be constrained.'[5] This note of rebellion in conjunction with an antipathy toward the rules and constraints of classicism are characteristic of the Spanish temperament and help to explain the overriding romantic quality that permeates Spanish literature as a whole. An extreme emphasis on individualism is illustrated by the quintessential affirmation of honour and pride that echoes throughout the *comedia*: 'yo soy yo' ('I am me'). This quality is combined with a strong sense of realism that is also characteristic of much of Spanish art and literature. The resultant fusion of disparate elements of style and content leads naturally to the grotesque,

---

[3] Paul Ilie, 'Bécquer and the Romantic grotesque', *PMLA*, 83, no. 2, 1968, p. 317.
[4] He has resided in Paris since 1955, but has become an increasing presence in Spain in the period following the death of the dictator Francisco Franco (1975).
[5] Geoffrey Harpham, *On the Grotesque Strategies of Contradiction in Art and Literature* (Princeton: Princeton University Press, 1982), p. 7.

which has been defined by Philip Thomson as 'the unresolved clash of incompatibles in work and response' (p. 27).

The grotesque is an aggressive artistic tool and aesthetic which is especially well suited to combatting socio-political abuses. As Roger Benoit notes: 'Artists, especially throughout the last century, have used the grotesque as a cudgel against political power and its predators.'[6] Goya, Valle-Inclán, Buñuel and Arrabal were certainly aware of its efficacy as a vehicle of protest. The clash between the people and the court, the ills of Spanish society, the horror of the French invasion and occupation and the tyranny of Fernando VII all inspired Goya's art. And Goya's pioneering use of the grotesque in his *Caprichos*, magnified by his incorporation of sarcastic and/or ironic captions and the dramatic nature of the scenes he depicted had a tremendous influence on the above mentioned artists. His black paintings and etchings for the *Disasters of War* and the *Disparates* are also replete with memorable examples of the grotesque, but for the purposes of this study only a few of the *Caprichos* will be considered.

An essential feature of the grotesque, noted by most of the critics who have attempted to analyze that aesthetic mode, is the union of human and animal elements. Goya's depiction of various characters either as animals or with animal-like features is a major characteristic of the *Caprichos*. Capricho 37, for example, depicts a teacher and his student as asses, and Goya's caption asks: 'Might not the pupil know more?'[7] The humorous element of the grotesque is further enhanced by showing the young animal studying the first letter of the alphabet, which reinforces his identity as an ass. Philip Thomson's view of the grotesque as the uneasy union of the horrifying and the comic is strikingly verified by Goya in a number of these etchings. Capricho 39 mocks the importance placed on one's lineage (and may be an oblique reference to the situation of Manuel de Godoy, the Queen María Luisa's lover). It presents another ass examining a book tracing his family tree, filled with pictures of other asses. The ludicrous smirk on his mouth and Goya's caption 'And so was his grandfather' add the final touch of black humour. Both black humour and the grotesque are inherently dialectical in nature and both are highly visual even when presented just in the form of written language.

Another powerful indictment of Spanish society at that time, with its pompous, immoral and shallow *majos* and *majas*, is contained in Capricho 19, with the caption 'All Will Fall'. The vacuous *majos* are

---

[6] Roger Benoit, 'The Grotesque in the Theater of Fernando Arrabal' (Diss. University of Kansas, 1975), p. 172.

[7] *Los caprichos*, Introduction Philip Hofer (New York: Dover Publications, 1969).

depicted as birds with human heads. When they do fall to earth, they are caught by a group of women, one of whom is a typical Goya character whose face is suggestive of an animal, and their feathers are plucked and their entrails removed.

Monks and other members of the church are frequently depicted as animal-like and faulted for their gluttony, avarice and oppressive fanaticism. One especially grotesque example would be Capricho 58 which shows a terrifying figure dressed in monk's garb with an animalesque face holding the apparatus for giving enemas as a frightened man pleads to be spared that treatment. The grotesque scene, effected in part by the scatalogical humour associated with that medical procedure, is further reinforced by Goya's caption 'Swallow it, Dog'.

Finally, Goya provides a whole series of caprichos showing young women being enticed into prostitution by animalesque old women. Capricho 17 shows just such an old hag examining the bared leg of a young woman and commenting: 'It is nicely stretched.' It is this type of scene that inspired Nigel Glendinning to observe in his study of Goya: 'The type of go-between or procuress is marvellously caught by Goya, who has the typically sharp eye for squalor that all Spanish artists have. You can imagine nothing more grotesquely repulsive, or more viciously deformed.'[8]

Goya's provocative series of etchings constitutes one of the most devastating satires of a society done by an artist. Many of the *Caprichos* utilize dramatic encounters between characters in a manner that is suggestive of the theatre. Priscilla Muller's observation about the nature of Goya's art serves to associate it with that genre and to provide a clear link to the dramas of Ramón del Valle-Inclán. She states: 'As his oeuvre demonstrates, Goya maintained a continuing interest in the many phenomena of the theater, from drama to sideshow. The fantasy world attainable in the theater, which grants temporary release from the normal limits of reality, is not unlike the world he created with the "black paintings", nor entirely unlike that ostensibly of sleep and reason which he revealed earlier in his *Caprichos*.'[9]

In his interesting study of Goya and his critics, Glendinning identifies a number of artists who were influenced by Goya's work. After stating that 'novelists, poets, dramatists and musicians, even stage designers and film directors, have been drawn to Goya's art or to his life' (p. 230), he says of Valle-Inclán that he 'valued the emotional quality of Goya's distortion and learnt much from it' (p. 236). Moreover, Valle-Inclán's

---

[8] Nigel Glendinning, *Goya and His Critics* (New Haven: Yale University Press, 1977), p. 79.
[9] Priscilla Muller, *Goya's Black Paintings* (New York: The Hispanic Society of America, 1984), p. 213.

dramaturgical art accorded unusual importance to visual elements and to the plastic arts. He is rightly regarded as a true pioneer of the theatre for his *esperpentos* of the 1920s, the essence of which is a visual deformation effected by holding a concave mirror up to the already grotesque distortion of a modern European society that was Spain. It is that aesthetic and the incorporation of the plastic arts into his stage directions and central concept of theatre that mark Valle-Inclán as a true innovator. As Sumner Greenfield notes: 'His aesthetic maintains that a work for the theater is as much a visual experience as a dramatic entity, and that the thematic content can be subordinated to the spectacle or to what is evoked aesthetically through the visual conception. Thus, his work is conceived not only as a dramatic form but also as a creation of plastic art.'[10]

Valle-Inclán was acutely aware of Goya's influence on his work, and affirmed it on a number of occasions. As Greenfield notes: 'Don Ramón makes it clear that the *esperpento* follows the grotesque tradition of Goya, and not the dehumanizing methods of contemporary *ultraísmo*' (p. 222). In Valle-Inclán's best-known *esperpento*, *Luces de bohemia*, his protagonist, Max Estrella, affirms Goya's influence in the text of the play itself, stating: 'It was Goya who invented the grotesque.'[11]

An in-depth study of Valle-Inclán's use of the grotesque lies beyond this study. A few observations about his most important plays and their role as a link between Goya, Buñuel and Arrabal will suffice to demonstrate his significant role in the development of a Spanish form of contemporary grotesque. In such plays as *Divinas palabras* (*Divine Words*) (1920) and *Luces de bohemia* (*Bohemian Lights*) (1924) Valle-Inclán's *Weltanschauung* relies so heavily on systematic and multi-faceted deformation that the grotesque becomes the central aesthetic of each. As Anthony Zahareas notes: 'The world of the *esperpento*s is consequently an unsettling world where tragedy and travesty exist side by side, while man's anguish and man's blundering are constantly played off against one another... In fact, *esperpento* is perhaps the first Spanish attempt to convert the loose and flexible machinery of the grotesque into an autonomous, aesthetic category.'[12]

---

[10] Sumner Greenfield, *Ramón del Valle-Inclán: Anatomía de un teatro problemático* (Madrid: Editorial Fundamentos, 1972), p. 23. This and all subsequent translations of critical material are my own.

[11] *Ramón del Valle-Inclán, Luces de Bohemia/Bohemian Lights*, trans. Anthony Zahareas and Gerald Gillespie (Austin: University of Texas Press, 1976), pp. 182–183.

[12] Anthony Zahareas, 'The Absurd, the Grotesque and the Esperpento', in *Ramón del Valle-Inclán: An Appraisal of His Life and Works*, ed. Anthony Zahareas (New York: Las Americas Publishing Co., 1968), p. 82.

Divinas palabras, a 'pre-esperpento', is an especially good example of a drama in which the dialogue and stage directions combine to produce a strikingly visual form of the grotesque that is central to the main theme of the work. Set in rural Galicia, the play constitutes a scathing denunciation of the cruelty and hypocrisy of the peasants inhabiting that area. The central figure in the play, who functions to expose the corruption and pharisaism dominant in the other characters, is the hydrocephalic dwarf, Laureano. This repulsive, disgusting, yet ultimately ludicrous and morbidly comic character is used for the purpose of begging; he is so hideous that even the callous populace of the area can be induced to give alms when he is propitiously displayed. He is on stage throughout almost the entire work and provides the drama with its central grotesque. Greenfield is clearly referring to Laureano when he makes the following comment about the play: 'Grotesque ugliness is the element that dominates the visual component of *Divine Words*, just as moral ignorance is the fundamental component of the characters' (p. 155). His statement is also suggestive of Goya, who frequently combined physical and moral horror with telling effect. The humorous dimension of Valle-Inclán's grotesque in *Divinas palabras* is produced by the conflation of Laureano's appearance, a virtual parody of the human form, and his assorted utterances, elicited by bribes of food and drink, often alcoholic in nature.

The child eventually dies from an excess of brandy. Mari-Gaila and Marica del Reino, the two sisters who care for the child on alternate days so each can profit from the alms he brings in, even attempt to delay his burial in order to earn a bit more charity. The stage directions that indicate how he is to be dressed for burial incorporate the disparate elements so characteristic of the grotesque; a detailed visual image describes the horror of the cadaver (its face had been largely devoured by pigs one night) in juxtaposition with the delicacy and beauty of the adorning trappings: 'The grotesque waxen head of the idiot, adorned with a crown of camellias, stands out against the white pillow. The rigid rotting corpse is covered in a blue shroud decorated with gold stars. On Laureano's stomach, swollen like that of a pregnant woman, lies a pewter dish filled with copper coins. At the very top of this pile of black coins lies a shiny peseta.'[13] Valle-Inclán's debt to the plastic arts is quite clear in his attention to pictorial detail and establishes the potential for the visual component of the grotesque in theatre, in the tradition of Goya and of the German Expressionist artist Georg Grosz.

---

[13] Ramón del Valle-Inclán, *Divine Words* in *Valle-Inclán Plays: One*, trans. Maria Delgado (London: Methuen, 1993), p. 76.

Luces de bohemia, Valle-Inclán's first bonafide *esperpento*, exhibits a somewhat different perspective on the part of the dramatist. The majority of the characters are archetypal Spaniards culled from the streets of Madrid who file past the spectator and constitute a grotesque composite of life in that city at the time of the play's composition. But the focal point and source of unity in the play is the blind poet, Max Estrella, whose consciousness of his grotesque nature elevates him above the level of the other characters. Zahareas summarizes the dialectical nature of the protagonist and the play in the following statement: 'For Max is the classic hero reflected mockingly in a concave mirror and at the same time the artist who envisions his own deformed mockery in the mirror of his mind. He is the tragic hero gesticulating like a puppet, and the classic artist converted into an indifferent puppeteer who sets down the grotesque formula of the *esperpento*. Simultaneously character and author, Max becomes the objective painter of his own ridiculous destiny.'[14]

A number of the characters of the drama, presented to the audience through the alcoholic vision of the protagonist, are described in the stage directions in terms of animals or puppets, giving the entire work a strong grotesque aesthetic. The King of Portugal, for example, is depicted as follows: 'An elongated and dirty tramp, newspaper vendor, smiles as he comes to the doorway, and like a dog in the act of delousing itself, shakes its shoulders jerkily, showing a great pock-marked smile.'[15] Hebe Campanella characterizes this sort of grotesque in a manner that links it clearly both to Goya and to Fernando Arrabal. He states: 'In the esperpentic work, the disordering of reality is achieved, above all, through automatism and deformation, characteristics of the satirical-grotesque ... The zoological characterization is a frequent technique in Valle-Inclán. With it he succeeds in debasing the human condition and achieving a distancing effect.'[16]

Even Max Estrella's death becomes a grotesque event lacking in dignity and traditional emotion. *Luces de bohemia* presents a nihilistic picture of Spain. The grotesque functions primarily as an artistic tool designed to communicate the author's view of social reality. Valle-Inclán's sensitivity to visual detail and fondness for stage directions reminiscent of the zoom lens technique in cinema suggest interesting possibilities for the utilization of film as a vehicle for the grotesque mode. The Spanish filmmaker whose use of the grotesque most closely links him with the tradition of Goya and Valle-Inclán is Luis Buñuel. Buñuel identified

---

[14] Anthony Zahareas, *Introduction to Bohemian Lights*, trans. Anthony Zahareas and Gerald Gillespie (Austin: University of Texas Press, 1976), p. 73.

[15] *Ibid.*, pp. 196–197.

[16] Hebe Noemí Campanella, *Valle-Inclán: Materia y forma del esperpento* (Buenos Aires: Epison Editora, 1980), p. 26.

strongly with Goya and even wrote a script for a film about that artist which was never made. As Glendinning notes in his book on Goya: 'Buñuel's personal involvement with his subject – sharing with Goya an Aragonese background, deafness and a belief in the freedom of the artist – make it a matter of regret that the film was never made. There are occasional references to Goya in some of Buñuel's films, and his *Phantom of Liberty* (1975) uses the fearful image of *The Third of May 1808* on more than one occasion' (p. 238). Francisco Aranda places Buñuel even more strongly in the tradition of the Spanish grotesque when he observes: 'Some of Buñuel's pictures – *L'Age d'or*, *Los Olvidados*, *Robinson Crusoe* and now *Nazarín* – without losing their cinematic quality, carry us to other provinces of the spirit; certain drawings by Goya, a poem by Quevedo or Péret, a chapter by the Marquis de Sade, a short play by Valle-Inclán, an episode by Cervantes.'[17] And, in the Introduction to her translation of three of Valle-Inclán's plays, Maria Delgado identifies dialectical forces in *Divinas palabras* as essential to 'the influence he has exerted over dramatists like Lorca and Arrabal as well as the filmmakers Luis Buñuel and Carlos Saura, similarly concerned with non-naturalistic modes of discourse'(pp. xxvii–xxviii).

Buñuel's grotesque often incorporates the surreal, aligning his art even further with Arrabal's. There are numerous grotesque scenes and figures in his films, from *An Andalusian Dog*, his collaboration with Salvador Dalí, to the dwarf Ujo in *Nazarín*, which inspired Virginia Higgenbotham to comment: 'Buñuel's love of the grotesque, as deeply rooted in Spanish art as in surrealism, is expressed in the figure of Ujo the dwarf.'[18] But undoubtedly his most famous and extensive use of the grotesque is in the film *Viridiana* (1961). In that work Viridiana, after leaving the convent, becomes a Christ-like benefactress for a group of beggars. She feeds and cares for the repulsive contingent, which includes a leper who is shunned by all of his peers. When she and her uncle's illegitimate son leave the estate one day, the beggars take over the home and prepare an extravagant dinner that deteriorates into a drunken orgy. The climax of the scene is the famous 'freeze-frame' in which one beggar, using her genitals as a camera, photographs the group in a pose that parodies Leonardo da Vinci's *Last Supper*. Black humour, visual grotesqueness and blasphemy all coalesce in that famous scene which Ado Kyrou categorizes as quintessentially Spanish when he states: 'the almost pornographic eroticism in blasphemy is characteristic of the Spanish spirit. Let us not forget that the richest, most splendid oaths are

---

[17] Francisco Aranda, *Luis Buñuel. A Critical Biography*, trans. David Robinson (New York: DaCapo Press, 1976), p. 179.
[18] Virginia Higgenbotham, *Luis Buñuel* (Boston: Twayne Publishers, 1979), p. 109.

Spanish.'[19] Kyrou's astute comment serves perfectly to link Buñuel with Arrabal, whose penchant for uniting blasphemy and the grotesque will be explored later in this study. And Higgenbotham brings Goya into the equation in the course of analyzing Buñuel's film *Tristana* (1969) when she states: 'Buñuel's last character study, *Tristana*, is his most savage, equaling Goya's *Caprichos* in the merciless rendering of hypocrisy and corruption' (p. 138). The playwright and filmmaker who assimilated these influences and, drawing upon the events of his traumatic childhood and subsequent experiences involving his native Spain, produced a corpus of works permeated by the grotesque is Fernando Arrabal.

Born in Melilla, Spanish Morocco in 1932, the harmony of Arrabal's early years was abruptly shattered by the outbreak of the Spanish Civil War on July 17, 1936. The ideological divison between the two Spains was echoed in his own family; his father was arrested and imprisoned by the Francoist forces whose agenda was strongly supported by his mother. Arrabal's early works reflect his conflicted feelings toward his mother, who dominated his entire childhood until he discovered his absent father when he came upon photos and letters hidden in the attic. Until then, his mother had forbidden any mention of her husband and had even excised his image from all photographs. It is not surprising, therefore, that Arrabal's theatre was categorized as absurdist by Martin Esslin in his landmark book on the theatre of the absurd,[20] or that the grotesque became a central aesthetic in his work. His first group of plays is peopled by childlike, amoral characters, who are often crushed by the absurd, incomprehensible macrocosmos that surrounds them and punishes their own cruel and grotesque acts. Harpham might have been describing Arrabal's peculiar brand of the grotesque when he observed that 'we have come to recognize that children are in many ways very like savages: children are intensely interested in the sensory, and especially intent on the alimentary and reproductive systems' (p. 66).

Arrabal's very first play, *Pic-Nic* (*Picnic on the Battlefield*) (1952), established the central role that the grotesque will play in so much of his theatre. The title itself incorporates the dialectical clash so essential to the grotesque. It demonstrates the type of black humour combined with horror that is central to the concept of the grotesque through the annoyance and frustration expressed by the stretcher-bearers when they fail to find an adequate supply of corpses on the battlefield. The childlike innocence of the soldiers Zapo and Zepo, the spoof of the institution of war and the comic nature of the parents who bring their picnic to the battlefield are suddenly subsumed by the violent destruction of all of

---

[19] Ado Kyrou, *Luis Buñuel* (New York: Simon Schuster, 1963), p. 96.
[20] Martin Esslin, *The Theater of the Absurd* (New York: Anchor Books, 1969), pp. 217–222.

those characters as reality obliterates the surreal, comic vision of the play.

The clash of opposites resulting from the naive, childlike tone of a work and the horror perpetrated by its ingenuous characters generates grotesque images in such plays as *El triciclo* (*The Tricycle*) (1953), *Fando y Lis* (*Fando and Lis*) (1956) and *Oración* (*Oraison*) (1957). But the early work that established most convincingly the grotesque as a provocative theatrical device is *Ceremonia por un negro asesinado* (*Ceremony for an Assasinated Black*) (1956). The play presents two vagabonds, Vincent and Jerome, who aspire to become stars of the theatre. They remain unperturbed by the cries of their neighbour, Luce, whose father has died. They also refuse to allow their own murder of the black man, Francis of Assisi (who had been slated to perform the leading role) to interfere with their plans to stage Shakespeare's *Othello*. In the second scene of the play they prepare Luce's father for burial, delighting in decorating his coffin, an act that they equate with stage design. In a grotesque funeral procession, they bedeck the cadaver in the costume of Cyrano de Bergerac, complete with a long, ridiculous nose. Here the grotesque functions to combat the horror of death by converting it into something both ludicrous and farcical. The tension between disparate forces that is so essential to the spirit of the grotesque is evident throughout the piece; the clash between the naiveté and simplicity of the childlike vagabonds and the horror of their deeds produces a pervasive tension and elicits a great deal of uneasy laughter from the audience.

The play's climactic scene demonstrates Arrabal's ability to utilize the grotesque in a highly visual and theatrical manner. Jerome, who suffered a stroke at the moment the black man was murdered, is now aphasic. The corpse has remained in the apartment for a week, and the resultant stench has aroused the ire of the neighbours. With the protestations of the latter audible in the background, Luce props up the paralyzed Jerome (his face now twisted into a permanent grimace) and delivers his lines for him as the trio of characters enacts a scene from *Othello*.

One of the characteristics of black humour, according to Gloria Orenstein, is 'the aesthetic and pleasurable appreciation of death and the glorification of cruelty, which provoke a sadistic humor that liberates the mind from all constraints of morality and propriety'.[21] The black humour in *Ceremonia por un negro asesinado* (*Ceremony for an Assassinated Black*) functions in just such a manner; its appeal to man's repressed infantile desires provides the element of the grotesque that balances the horror of the play. Even the arrival of the police at the play's conclusion fails to

---

[21] Gloria Orenstein, *The Theater of the Marvelous* (New York: New York University Press, 1975), pp. 155–156.

dissipate the contagious euphoria experienced by the characters during their rendition of the scene from *Othello*. Arrabal's grotesque, then, demonstrates the potential for a theatre that utilizes black humour to free itself from the shackles of outmoded and restrictive dramatic conventions.

Arrabal's theatre acquires its uniqueness through the fusion of a very Spanish form of black humour and the grotesque with the avant-garde currents he encountered and assimilated after his self-imposed exile to France in 1955. The Surrealists, the experimental directors like Víctor García, Jorge Lavelli and Jerôme Savary, and a whole group of artists and writers encouraged him to expand upon his Spanish sensibility and to incorporate a number of forms of art into his theatre. As a result, Arrabal became the most successful dramatist in his implementation of the theories of Antonin Artaud, expressed in his famous treatise *The Theater and its Double*.[22] A by-product of the development of his *gesamtkuntswerk* was a corollary expansion of the nature and role of the grotesque in his theatre. As Roger Benoit notes, 'the grotesque finds room to breathe, and flourishes in a theatre where a variety of art forms are nourished' (p. 64). Sound effects, the use of slides, the incorporation of the audience into the stage space and action of the work, music, movement and gesture eradicated traditional boundaries between audience and actors and effected a true Artaudian assault on the senses of the public. Víctor García's famous production of *El cementerio de automóviles* (*The Car Cemetery*) (1957) which incorporated several other Arrabal plays and which was staged in Dijon, France, in 1966, inspired the playwright to explore further the possibilities for expanding the traditional use of stage space in his theatre. A constant throughout many of his dramas which facilitated an expanding use of both the grotesque and avant-garde theatre techniques was the role of ceremony in the conception of his plays. Benoit comments that 'it is ceremony, ritual, feast, sacrilege, sacredness, life and death which all blend into a poetry which I have identified as the "Arrabalesque grotesque"'(p. 42). Examples of the use of ceremony in Arrabal's theatre abound. For the purposes of this study, the brief play *Primera comunión* (*Solemn Communion*) (1963) will be considered as a prelude to the longer, more complex *El Arquitecto y el Emperador de Asiria* (*The Architect and the Emperor of Assyria*) (1965).

One structuring device in *Primera comunión* (*Solemn Communion*) involves a young girl's preparations for a landmark religious ceremony. She gets dressed for that event throughout much of the short play, aided by her grandmother, who lectures her incessantly on the virtues of being a dutiful wife and model homemaker. The conversation is interrupted

---

[22] Antonin Artaud, *The Theater and its Double*, trans. Mary Caroline Richards (New York: Grove Press, 1958).

repeatedly by the appearance of a necrophiliac pursuing a coffin containing a deceased young woman. The grotesque emerges from the interplay of the horror of this exceptionally loathsome perversion and the humour derived from the tone of the work, the naivité of the girl, and the baroque nature of the communicant's costume and of the necrophiliac's sex organ, which takes the form of a snake of ever-increasing length. The intermittent appearances of the necrophiliac also give structure to the play, infusing it with a growing dramatic tension that culminates in the girl's stabbing the necrophiliac repeatedly after he has entered the coffin and begun to make love to the corpse. Blood then spatters on her communion dress. She has, in a sense, affirmed her sexuality, but the insidious quality inherent in the grandmother's cliché-ridden advice has not been without effect. Arrabal heightens the grotesque quality of the scene by interjecting the incongruous visual effect of red balloons ascending from the coffin after the girl has stabbed the sexual deviate. This 'playful' little touch combines with the overall horror of the piece to produce a grotesque image that unites religion and a perverse kind of sexual florescence and has as its ultimate objective the exposure of the equally grotesque nature of the Spanish upbringing. This work is just one of many theatre ceremonies that caused Benoit to observe that 'the playwright's iconoclastic jabbing must be further characterized as being peculiarly Catholic and Spanish in flavour, roughly similar in kind to the mock supper in Buñuel's *Viridiana*' (pp. 114–115).

Arrabal continued to explore the possibilities of ceremony and to expand his artistic vocabulary in works like *El gran ceremonial* (*The Grand Ceremonial*) (1963) and *Ars Amandi* (*The Art of Love*) (1968). The latter is an opera that uses music, dance, mannequins and the projection of slides of art works by painters such as Goya, Bosch and Max Ernst. But the work of this period, generally referred to as his 'Panic theatre', which has emerged as his true masterpiece is *El Arquitecto y el Emperador de Asiria* (*The Architect and the Emperor of Assyria*). In that drama, rich in visual and auditory stimuli and cyclical in structure as are so many of Arrabal's plays, the Emperor's search for psychic unity, his need for the other (the Architect), his participation in numerous role-playing games designed to allow him both to escape from and to draw closer to the image of his mother, and the grotesque pomposity which masks his psychological frailty all coalesce in the drama's climactic scene. The Emperor's trial, his ultimate game, fuses with the reality of his psychic existence. At its conclusion he orders the Architect to kill him, and then devour him while dressed in the clothes of the Emperor's mother.

This symbolic surrender to the spirit of that parent is also a form of retribution for the Emperor's murder of her (be it real or merely subconscious). The grotesque scene in which the Architect carries out his companion's final command and assumes his identity upon completion of the 'feast' combines humour, scatology, blasphemy (the parody of the

Transubstantiation), and intense human emotion into a supremely theatrical act that affirms the union of the base and the exalted on a mythical level.

The incorporation of a sequence in which the Emperor, dressed as a woman, attempts to prove the existence of God by playing pinball, games and rituals which involve a pregnant nun giving birth and blasphemies equating God and excrement sung loudly by the Emperor resonate with human psychology and a profound exploration of the nature of the human condition. As Diana Taylor notes in her introduction to the play: 'the discrepancies and insanities provide an inexhaustible source of black humor in the work which continuously amuses and shocks us, catches us unawares, and bombards us with almost desperate comedy, all part of an electrifying theatrical experience.'[23] The grotesque in Arrabal, then, performs a myriad of functions, from the deformation of an already caricaturesque social reality in the spirit of Valle-Inclán to the nightmarish depiction and partial resolution of the artist's and of mankind's deep-seated inner conflicts and obsessions.

Arrabal's experiences in a Spanish jail cell in 1967 inspired a number of more overtly political works that utilized the grotesque in telling fashion to protest conditions in his native Spain. *Y pondrán esposas en las flores* (*And They Put Handcuffs on the Flowers*) (1969) sought to plunge the audience into the grotesque milieu of a Spanish prison. As the spectators arrived, they were to be accosted by the cast, separated from their companions, verbally and physically abused by actors, and ultimately encouraged to participate actively in the spectacle. In that drama, dream sequences are juxtaposed with realistic horrors. A central sequence emerges featuring the futile appeal of the victimized prisoner Tosan, who is ultimately garroted as a series of government and church officials decline to save him, rubbing their hands in a bowl of blood and wiping them on a white flag that becomes an extremely powerful visual prop. The sequence in which a prisoner's wife (an allusion to Arrabal's mother) dances 'The Dying Swan' while her husband is tortured illustrates the playwright's penchant for visual black humour. An especially striking grotesque sequence involves the blinding and castration of a sadistic priest. The horror of what has been done to him is immediately tempered by the humour of his scatological prayer, uttered reverently while he unctuously chews his own testicles. That image and several other grotesqueries found their way into Arrabal's first film, *Viva la muerte* (*Long Live Death*) (1971) in which the artist explored the possibilities for expanding his visual grotesqueries in another medium.

---

[23] Diana Taylor, *Introduction to El Arquitecto y el Emperador de Asiria* (Madrid: Cátedra, 1984), p. 59.

In recent years, while continuing to write for the theatre, Arrabal has produced an increasing number of works in other genres such as painting, film, novels and essays. In keeping with the focus on drama, this study will conclude with a brief consideration of his first play to enjoy commercial and artistic success in his native Spain, *Oye, patria, mi aflicción* (*Hear, My Country, My Affliction*) (1975). In this play, Arrabal unites his expanding repertoire of visual, cinematographic effects with his highly subjective, grotesque vision of a number of prominent literary and historical figures culled from Spain's past. The result is a strong affirmation of the vitality of his Spanish sensibility, reflected in both his choice of themes and his dramatic technique. There is a definite resonance between the dramatist's affliction, or pain, and his country's. The play's protagonist is Latidia, the Duchess of Teran (the surname of Arrabal's own mother). The fanciful and the grotesque figures and events that constitute the heart of the play may then be viewed as subjective projections of the dreams and obsessions of that protagonist.

Arrabal had previously translated the nightmares that dominated the inner world of his protagonist into a dazzling array of images in his film *Viva la muerte*. That work in the medium of film served him particularly well in *Oye, patria, mi aflicción*. The fourth scene of the play, in which Latidia passes in review before the mummies of the greats of Spanish history while wearing a gas mask to avoid their rank odour, constitutes a quintessential grotesque image strongly suggestive of the world of cinema. Luis Buñuel and his masterpiece *Viridiana* are specifically alluded to in another scene in which three beggars, having assumed the identities of El Cid, Che Guevara and Don Juan, participate in a grotesque banquet. Arrabal's sense of irony and sarcasm has never been stronger than in this evocation of the decadence that has consumed Spain and undermined and distorted the highest achievements of her past great figures.

The central episode of *Oye, patria, mi aflicción* concerns Latidia's efforts to retain her castle, which has been sold. Arrabal ironically undermines her heroic struggle to hold onto the past, however, through the repeated motif of the termites which gradually destroy the castle from within. Images of putrefaction recur throughout the work and serve to make a powerful statement about the dramatist's view of the state of his native land. Past traditions are ruthlessly mocked in scenes where Saint Theresa, Cervantes, El Cid and his wife, Jimena, and other historical notables engage in sado-masochistic acts. These violent aberrations prompted the critic Enrique Llovera[24] to link Arrabal's vision of Spanish

---

[24] Enrique Llovera, 'La aflicción de Arrabal, oída', *Estafeta literaria*, 639, 1 July 1978, p. 6.

myths with Valle-Inclán's *esperpentos*. The play ends optimistically as the collapse of the Castle is quickly followed by the rise of the Tower of Babel, which comes to symbolize harmony and renewal. The strong emphasis on stage pictures and a highly visual sense of the grotesque affirm Arrabal's continuing debt to Goya, Valle-Inclán and Buñuel in this work.

To state that there is a grotesque that is uniquely Spanish is probably somewhat of an exaggeration. Dark humour, extravagant blasphemy, and the systematic deformation of an already grotesque reality are qualities that are not limited exclusively to works of art, literature and film produced in Spain. However, that country certainly occupies a primary position today among the nations whose finest artists and writers have resorted to the grotesque in an attempt to identify an aesthetic uniquely appropriate for the expression of their psychological and sociological concerns. Fernando Arrabal's corpus illustrates more clearly than perhaps any other the full range of possibilities for the grotesque. And his extensive utilization of that aesthetic aligns him with a number of Spain's greatest writers and artists and affirms very clearly his debt to Francisco de Goya, to Ramón del Valle-Inclán and to Luis Buñuel.

Contemporary Theatre Review
1998, Vol. 7, Part 3, pp. 109–110
Reprints available directly from the publisher
Photocopying permitted by license only

Notes on Contributors

Maria M. Delgado is a lecturer in Drama at Queen Mary and Westfield College, the University of London. She is co-editor of the recent *In contact with the gods?: Directors talk theatre* (Manchester: Manchester University Press, 1996), and editor of *Valle-Inclán Plays: One* (London: Methuen, 1993). She is author of numerous articles on Hispanic and British theatre and Spanish film, co-programmer of the Manchester Spanish Film Festival, a Drama Advisor for North West Arts, and an advisor to the London film festival. She is currently working on two books with the American director Peter Sellars.

John London works in the School of European Languages, University of Wales, Swansea. He has translated plays by Federico García Lorca, Sergi Belbel, Joan Brossa, Rodolf Sirera, and José Sanchis Sinisterra. His other publications include *El teatre de la pàgina* (1993), *Great Theatres of the World* (1994) and *Reception and Renewal in Modern Spanish Theatre: 1939–1963* (1997). Together with David George, he has edited *Contemporary Catalan Theatre: An Introduction* (1996).

Peter L. Podol is a professor of Spanish at Lock Haven University in Pennsylvania. The author of the Twayne book on Fernando Arrabal, he has edited Arrabal's play *And They Put Handcuffs on the Flowers* in Spanish and published numerous articles in the field of contemporary Spanish theatre. He has also contributed essays on contemporary theatre to several books, served as bibliographer and member of the editorial board of the journal *Estreno*, and participated with his students at Lock Haven in the production and staging of one-act plays in Spanish.

Stephen G. H. Roberts is a lecturer in Hispanic Studies at the University of Nottingham. He has published on twentieth-century Spanish literature and film and is currently researching a book on Miguel de Unamuno's experience of exile in the 1920s.

María Francisca Vilches de Frutos is a full-time researcher on the Chief Board of Scientific Research in Madrid and advisor to the Cultural Minister. Since 1984 she has headed the research project 'The theatre history of Madrid between 1900 and 1936: Text and Presentation' sponsored by the Spanish Ministry of Education. In 1993 she became Co-director of the review *Annals of Contemporary Spanish Literature. Drama/Theatre*, published at Boulder University Colorado (USA). The author of numerous books and articles on the contemporary theatre, she recently published, in collaboration with Dru Dougherty, *La escena Madrileña Entre 1918 y 1926: Análisis y documentación* (1990) and *El teatro en España entre la tradición y la vanguardia: 1918–1939* (1992). She is currently completing her new book *Theatre and Democracy: The Madrid Scene between 1982 and 1995.*

Contemporary Theatre Review
1998, Vol. 7, Part 3, pp. 111–116
Reprints available directly from the publisher
Photocopying permitted by license only

© 1998 OPA (Overseas Publishers Association)
Amsterdam B.V. Published under license
under the Harwood Academic Publishers imprint,
part of The Gordon and Breach Publishing Group.
Printed in India.

Index

Plays are listed by author and films are listed by title. Devised pieces are listed under the name of the company or director who produced them. I refer to the main text only and not to the notes:

CONTEMPORARY THEATRE REVIEW
AN INTERNATIONAL JOURNAL

Notes for contributors

Submission of a paper will be taken to imply that it represents original work not previously published, that it is not being considered for publication elsewhere and that, if accepted for publication, it will not be published elsewhere in the same form, in any language, without the consent of editor and publisher. It is a condition of acceptance by the editor of a typescript for publication that the publisher automatically acquires the copyright of the typescript throughout the world. It will also be assumed that the author has obtained all necessary permissions to include in the paper items such as quotations, musical examples, figures, tables etc. Permissions should be paid for prior to submission.

Typescripts. Papers should be submitted in triplicate to the Editors, *Contemporary Theatre Review*, c/o Harwood Academic Publishers, at:

5th Floor, Reading Bridge House	820 Town Center Drive	3-14-9, Okubo
Reading Bridge Approach	Langhorne	Shinjuku-ku
Reading RGl 8PP or	PA 19047 USA or	Tokyo 169
UK		Japan

Papers should be typed or word processed with double spacing on one side of good quality ISO A4 (212 × 297 mm) paper with a 3 cm left-hand margin. Papers are accepted only in English.

Abstracts and Keywords. Each paper requires an abstract of 100–150 words summarizing the significant coverage and findings, presented on a separate sheet of paper. Abstracts should be followed by up to six key words or phrases which, between them, should indicate the subject matter of the paper. These will be used for indexing and data retrieval purposes.

Figures. All figures (photographs, schema, charts, diagrams and graphs) should be numbered with consecutive arabic numerals, have descriptive captions and be mentioned in the text. Figures should be kept separate from the text but an approximate position for each should be indicated in the margin of the typescript. It is the author's responsibility to obtain permission for any reproduction from other sources.

Preparation: Line drawings must be of a high enough standard for direct reproduction; photocopies are not acceptable. They should be prepared in black (india) ink on white art paper, card or tracing paper, with all the lettering and symbols included. Computer-generated graphics of a similar high quality are also acceptable, as are good sharp photoprints ("glossies"). Computer print-outs must be completely legible. Photographs intended for halftone reproduction must be good glossy original prints of maximum contrast. Redrawing or retouching of unusable figures will be charged to authors.

Size: Figures should be planned so that they reduce to 12 cm column width. The preferred width of line drawings is 24 cm, with capital lettering 4 mm high, for reduction by one-half. Photographs for halftone reproduction should be approximately twice the desired finished size.

Captions: A list of figure captions, with the relevant figure numbers, should be typed on a separate sheet of paper and included with the typescript.

Musical examples: Musical examples should be designated as "Figure 1" etc., and the recommendations above for preparation and sizing should be followed. Examples must be well prepared and of a high standard for reproduction, as they will not be redrawn or retouched by the printer.

In the case of large scores, musical examples will have to be reduced in size and so some clarity will be lost. This should be borne in mind especially with orchestral scores.

Notes are indicated by superior arabic numerals without parentheses. The text of the notes should be collected at the end of the paper.

References are indicated in the text by the name and date system either "Recent work (Smith & Jones, 1987, Robinson, 1985, 1987) . . ." or "Recently Smith & Jones (1987) . . ." If a publication has more than three authors, list all names on the first occurrence; on subsequent occurrences use the first author's name plus "*et al.*" Use an ampersand rather than "and" between the last two authors. If there is more than one publication by the same author(s) in the same year, distinguish by adding a, b, c etc. to both the text citation and the list of references (e.g. "Smith, 1986a") References should be collected and typed in alphabetical order after the Notes and Acknowledgements sections (if these exist). Examples:

Benedetti, J. (1988) *Stanislavski*, London: Methuen

Granville-Barker, H. (1934) Shakespeare's dramatic art. In *A Companion to Shakespeare Studies*, edited by H. Granville-Barker and G. B. Harrison, p. 84. Cambridge: Cambridge University Press

Johnston, D. (1970) Policy in theatre. *Hibernia*, **16**, 16

Proofs. Authors will receive page proofs (including figures) by air mail for correction and these must be returned as instructed within 48 hours of receipt. Please ensure that a full postal address is given on the first page of the typescript so that proofs are not delayed in the post. Authors' alterations, other than those of a typographical nature, in excess of 10% of the original composition cost, will be charged to authors.

Page Charges. There are no page charges to individuals or institutions.

INSTRUCTIONS FOR AUTHORS

ARTICLE SUBMISSION ON DISK

The Publisher welcomes submissions on disk. The instructions that follow are intended for use by authors whose articles have been accepted for publication and are in final form. Your adherence to these guidelines will facilitate the processing of your disk by the typesetter. These instructions do not replace the journal Notes for Contributors; all information in Notes for Contributors remains in effect.

When typing your article, do not include design or formatting information. Type all text flush left, unjustified and without hyphenation. Do not use indents, tabs or multi-spacing. If an indent is required, please note it by a line space; also mark the position of the indent on the hard copy manuscript. Indicate the beginning of a new paragraph by typing a line space. Leave one space at the end of a sentence, after a comma or other punctuation mark, and before an opening parenthesis. Be sure not to confuse lower case letter "l" with numeral "1", or capital letter "O" with numeral "0". Distinguish opening quotes from close quotes. Do not use automatic page numbering or running heads.

Tables and displayed equations may have to be rekeyed by the typesetter from your hard copy manuscript. Refer to the journal Notes for Contributors for style for Greek characters, variables, vectors, etc.

Articles prepared on most word processors are acceptable. If you have imported equations and/or scientific symbols into your article from another program, please provide details of the program used and the procedures you followed. If you have used macros that you have created, please include them as well.

You may supply illustrations that are available in an electronic format on a separate disk. Please clearly indicate on the disk the file format and/or program used to produce them, and supply a high-quality hard copy of each illustration as well.

Submit your disk when you submit your final hard copy manuscript. The disk file and hard copy must match exactly.

If you are submitting more than one disk, please number each disk. Please mark each disk with the journal title, author name, abbreviated article title and file names.

Be sure to retain a back-up copy of each disk submitted. Pack your disk carefully to avoid damage in shipping, and submit it with your hard copy manuscript and complete Disk Specifications form (see reverse) to the person designated in the journal Notes for Contributors.

Disk Specifications

Journal name _____

_____

Date _____ **Paper Reference Number** _____

Paper title _____

_____

_____

Corresponding author _____

Address _____

_____

_____

_____ **Postcode** _____

Telephone _____

Fax _____

E-mail _____

Disks Enclosed (file names and descriptions of contents)

Text

Disk 1 _____

Disk 2 _____

Disk 3 _____

PLEASE RETAIN A BACK-UP COPY OF ALL DISK FILES SUBMITTED.

GORDON AND BREACH PUBLISHERS   •   HARWOOD ACADEMIC PUBLISHERS

Figures

Disk 1 _____

Disk 2 _____

Disk 3 _____

Computer make and model _____

_____

Size/format of floppy disks

☐ 3.5"   ☐ 5.25"

☐ Single sided   ☐ Double sided

☐ Single density ☐ Double density   ☐ High density

Operating system _____

Version _____

Word processor program _____

Version _____

Imported maths/science program _____

Version _____

Graphics program _____

Version _____

Files have been saved in the following format

Text: _____

Figures: _____

Maths: _____

PLEASE RETAIN A BACK-UP COPY OF ALL DISK FILES SUBMITTED.

GORDON AND BREACH PUBLISHERS   ●   **HARWOOD ACADEMIC PUBLISHERS**